UNLIMIT YOUR LIFE

James Fadiman, Ph.D.

UNLIMIT YOUR LIFE

▲▲————————————————▲▲

Setting & Getting Goals

CELESTIALARTS

Berkeley, California

CELESTIAL ARTS
P.O. Box 7327
Berkeley, California 94707

Cover design by Ken Scott
Text design by Nancy Austin
Composition by HMS Typography, Inc.

Library of Congress Cataloging-in-Publication Data

Fadiman, James, 1939–
    Unlimit your life : setting and getting goals / James
Fadiman.
        p.   cm.
    Bibliography: p.
    Includes index.
    ISBN 0-89087-562-6
    1. Success.   I. Title.
BJ1611.2.F33   1989
158'.1—dc20   89-31702
                                                      CIP

First Printing, 1989
1 2 3 4 — 91 90 89

Manufactured in the United States of America

TO

John Boyle

Whose life was committed to giving to others and whose work restored to many the opportunities they had thought lost. John taught that there is always more available for those who choose it. He exemplified this in his generosity, his zest for life and his dedication to helping others achieve their goals.

TO

Helen Boyle

Whose wisdom, kindness and good nature nurtured and supported me. Helen's understanding and myriad contributions cannot be counted; they are a continual string of blessings which kept the work always focused in service and on love.

ACKNOWLEDGMENTS

Writing can be a lonely pursuit, but it is never a solitary task.

I am indebted to the editing skills and endless good will of Richard Lukin who reworked my original prose back into English, and created order where there was none. His clarity and attention to detail made this manuscript far more lucid. The errors remaining are all my own.

The ideas in Chapters VII and VIII are derived from the work of James Adams, and Robert McKim of Stanford University. Special thanks to Tom Osborne and the staff of the Federal Home Loan Bank of Seattle, and to Joanna Weichert and many employees of Tandem Computers who helped in the development of the material in Chapter XII.

I am also grateful to those friends, clients and members of my family, especially Dorothy, my wife, who allowed me the time and the privacy that I needed to write at all.

Most of all, I am grateful to the openness of those who have shared their lives with me. Seeing the success in your lives inspired me to write this book.

An earlier version of much of this material was published for Omega Seminars, Inc. as *Be All That You Are*.

CONTENTS

INTRODUCTION

This is a book about regaining your freedom by controlling the basic forces which dominate your life. It is a guide to revitalizing potentials within yourself which, through no fault of your own, may have been closed down earlier in your life.

If your attempts to improve your life have up to now met with only slight success, this book will help you understand and resolve whatever seems to be standing in your way. Taking total control of one's life takes determination and information. The information presented here is meant to encourage you to continue to develop your own path.

Taking control of your life means perceiving the relationships between your early history, your current mind-set, and your self-imposed limitations. This book will help you gain that necessary understanding. No one system owns the truth. But, as a companion to almost all of them, this book can serve as a foundation for more specialized techniques which you may learn or may currently be practicing.

Freedom and a life that works are not to be thought of as reserved for the fortunate few. They are your birthright. I've included many examples of transformations, drawn from people

I have known and worked with in seminars, counseling sessions, and classes in universities, industry, government, and growth centers. People everywhere can and do change their lives.

Do not lose heart.

I

ESTABLISHING GOALS

*Anything you may hold firmly
in your imagination,
can be yours.*

—WILLIAM JAMES

**Without goals, you become
what you were.
With goals, you become what you wish.**

W ith seasonal regularity, each year a crop of self-help books and tapes are produced that teach that setting goals, visualizing them and saying affirmations about them are the keys to the kingdom.

And they are.

Yet most people who read the books or listen to or watch the tapes fail to achieve their goals. Most of these works, however skillfully presented, treat only one symptom or another without probing into the underlying causes or adequately describing the underlying cure. All too often, the authors assume that the hard basic work to achieve sufficient insight has already been accomplished. Ironically, it takes no more effort to have one's life work well than it does to have it flounder, yet most of us put as much effort into maintaining problems as is required to solve them. It does not take additional energy to improve one's life, just a redirection of effort into more profitable channels.

The aim of this book is to ensure that you will set goals *correctly for yourself* and to help you to understand, *on your own terms,* what rests between you and your goals, as well as how to overcome these individual obstacles.

Let's start at the beginning. To set goals means to set a course for your life. Like the captain of a sailing boat who sets a course—toward any desired port—using the wind, regardless of its strength or direction. With your course set, you experience daily progress—sometimes direct, sometimes indirect, but always moving in the direction of your ultimate destination.

Most of us don't decide what direction we are going nor how we will get there. We live from day to day, doing what needs to be done, enjoying what we can, regretting what we've missed. Most people cope . . . get by . . . adjust. Passive, accepting, and reactive to their world instead of choosing and creating it. They live in a rowboat with no oars—and no rudder. They move from place to place, but it is the winds and the currents that set the direction.

There are philosophies which indeed support this choice of lifestyle (for it is, most certainly, a choice). In spiritual circles people say "go with the flow." In business settings, people say "don't rock the boat." In the animal kingdom, there are whole species with few goals beyond survival, and they survive. Jellyfish are a group without goals; wholly passive, they *literally* drift with the currents. When food passes close to them, they eat; otherwise, they don't. Their life cycle is an example of coping, of living with minimal goals, and yet they have lasted millions of years and are one of the oldest unchanged species on the planet.

We are, however, beings-in-process; *we are changing, whether we realize it or not.* We are capable of leading *active* rather than *passive* lives. Jellyfish cannot decide their goals, and cannot make choices. It is healthier to have conscious goals—for our lives offer opportunities beyond drifting. To set goals is to benefit from our advantages.

We tend to see ourselves as having a constant identity, yet we are actually continuously changing. Even at the cellular level, we are in a continuous, gradual process of transformation, losing and replacing millions of cells each day. The surface of our skin is new every week, the tissue of our throat every few days. Over a period of years, every single cell except for some brain tissue is replaced.

If you reflect on your interests and ideas, you will notice that they too undergo gradual replacement through internal changes, shifts, and new orientations. Like trees which drop their leaves each winter to emerge with new ones in the spring, we are forever in the process of changing our attitudes and our understanding.

To establish goals is to direct the changes. We have no choice but to age, but we can choose the ways in which we will grow older. We can choose to have better health or worse; more freedom or less; greater income or less; more relationships or fewer.

Maurice Maeterlinck, the Nobel prize winning author, summed it up: "Those men who are more developed are aware of their destiny. They are familiar with their future because they are already part of their future." *Those who set goals create their own futures.*

BASIC GOALS

Certain goals appear to be necessary and basic for each of us. These include:

The Willingness to Be Happy

This is the fundamental note to which our lives are tuned. It requires that one be unwilling to suffer passively—to reject defeat, limitation, weakness, stupidity, or illness as much as you are able.

Being willing to be happy means accepting the idea that *you deserve happiness*. To deserve happiness is to have a self-concept which cherishes your fundamental worth, notwithstanding your current and past problems, defects, and deficiencies. It includes an awareness of your potential, your talents, and your capacities. Being willing to be happy is not being happy, but it consciously establishes your happiness as a goal. It supports the tree that sprouts from the seed of self-acceptance.

Increasing the Capacity to Love

Only those who are able to love are fully human, are fully alive. Once you make the commitment to personal happiness, then a natural expression of that happiness is to take pleasure in being with other people.

As happiness breeds happiness, so love and affection breed more love and affection. As children we may have been starved for love; we may have been frightened by people or experiences and thus thwarted in expressing it. As part of a couple we may fear not receiving it. As parents we may not feel comfortable in giving it. As friends we may feel inhibited in expressing it.

It is critical to improve our capacity to love. But out of the rough-and-tumble of childhood, many of us emerged scared, embittered, cautious, unskilled, or deficient in this natural capacity. We may confuse love with respect, with obedience, with guilt, with sex, with power. A necessary basic goal is to expand our willingness and capacity to love. Like taking water from a bubbling well, giving love to others in abundance does not diminish the supply.

Enjoyable Work

Since we all do something, we might as well enjoy it. Paid or not, we spend more time working than in all our other activities. It has been shown, in countless studies, that work satisfaction is a major life issue. We are happy when we are productive and when we are productive we are likely to be happy.

Here are two question about your relationship to your work. *Do you look forward to getting down to work? Do you feel you have done a good job by day's end?* If both your answers are "yes," then you are already succeeding in this arena. If either of your answers are "no," then you still have goals to set and goals to achieve.

Salary or income is usually part of work satisfaction. It is important that you earn enough so that you feel worthwhile, whatever that figure may be. Research has shown that there is almost no correlation between work satisfaction and wages as long as the wages are reasonable for the job in question. What you do matters—that you enjoy it matters even more.

Good Health

There is nothing so central as the appreciation of our own well-being. Some years ago I was in a serious car collision and spent the subsequent five months in bed. I couldn't work or fulfill other obligations; I was preoccupied with my health. I observed that I lost none of my willingness to be happy. The accident, if anything, strengthened my determination. During my recovery, I stumbled onto opportunities for happiness that my usual busy, active life had obscured. Also, I lost none of my desire to love others. For the first time, I had the leisure to see how vital it was to my own well-being and to theirs. I came to know that without good health, my other goals—financial, social and professional—lost their savor.

As one's willingness to be happy increases, goals for personal health are set higher and higher. A doctor once told me,

"I'll work with you and help you to get healthier. When you feel you're healthy enough; when you feel that you can't improve any more, then you can stop doing whatever we've agreed on." What he was teaching me was that my goal should not end with "no illness," but should envision, always, better health.

Physical fitness experts all agree on three basic requirements for good health:

1. A diet that supports the proper nourishment of each cell, each organ, and the whole body.

2. Exercise that stimulates and improves circulation.

3. The ability to relax and to recover from stress.

Illness can cast a fog over our lives. When we recover, there seems to be more light, and we increasingly enjoy each task we undertake. When every part of the body hums with good health, it needs no further definition, no intellectual understanding.

Inner Integrity

Inner integrity is a subtle yet vital goal. It includes having more control over your own life without the need to change or restrict the lives of those around you. The need to control others often arises out of fear—fear that we will get less, will not be accepted, will lose love, or be passed over. While the ability to successfully control others may be a strength, the need to do so is almost always a defense.

Manipulating others conflicts with other basic goals, and the effort may express itself as headaches, stomach problems, high blood pressure, and heart conditions. Trying to manipulate the world so that it won't harm us forecloses on love. We cannot love those whom we guard against. We still love, but it is with one arm stretched out to embrace and the other ready to push away. Controlling others can rob us of inner joy. When we operate without respect for our capacity to face others openly and clearly, we operate from weakness and diminish ourselves.

Inner integrity does not connote speaking out every thought or feeling that comes into our head, nor allowing ourselves to be pushed around. Inner integrity increases our capacity to achieve what we wish in this world without limiting anyone else's opportunities, and reminds us that reinforcing the inner integrity of others makes them our allies. At work we can delegate responsibility effectively; at home we encourage everyone to be himself or herself.

It is from the foundation of these five basic goals that our fluctuating personal, private goals emerge. Before we look at individual goals, let us look at some of the personal characteristics of extremely successful people.

SELF-ACTUALIZERS

The psychologist Abraham Maslow helped clarify the pivotal elements in people who have made remarkable progress within their own lives. He called these people "self-actualizers," a term he coined to describe those who appear to have obtained the highest and finest goals to which we all aspire. He studied the brightest, the kindest, the most creative and talented people he could find. He asked them to nominate the most fully developed and impressive people they knew. He then explored and researched the lifestyles and values of that group, trying to identify their best qualities.

Over the years he began to recognize certain patterns in these "self-actualized" individuals: they made "full use of talents, capacities, potentialities, etc." He concluded that the self-actualizing person is "not an ordinary person with something added, but rather, the ordinary person with nothing taken away. The average person is a full human being with dampened and inhibited powers and capacities." Self-actualizing people see life clearly. They are objective, and are unlikely to allow hopes, fears, or defenses to distort their perception. They are committed to something greater than themselves, and tend to do well at their chosen tasks. They work hard, and are spontaneous, creative, and courageous in their daily lives.

Self-actualizers enjoy and appreciate life more than most. They have their normal share of pain, sorrow, and disappointments, but they have more interests and get more pleasure out of life. They are more resilient, and experience less fear, anxiety, boredom, and purposelessness. They are keenly aware of beauty and appreciate it over and over—in a sunrise, in nature, in their marriage. While most of us enjoy only occasional moments of joy or "peak experience," self-actualizers seem to love life in general, enjoying all its aspects.

Self-actualizers, by Maslow's definition, are relatively free of neurosis and make excellent use of their innate talents and capacities. They are far from perfect, however. These "very same people can be at times boring, irritating, petulant, selfish, angry, or depressed." Our so-called natural limits maybe then are actually unnatural—common, usual, typical, but not necessarily valid. They do not originate from the core of our being.

INDIVIDUAL GOALS

There are basic goals which seem appropriate for everyone, but how you make your life work is personal, unique, and individual. It's easy to become so infatuated with the higher abstract visions that we neglect the practical opportunities that surround us every day.

Individual goals can be divided into two forms: tangible—income, assets, houses, boats, planes, horses, farms, gardens, furniture; and intangible—health, skills, relationships, leisure, and self-confidence and the like. The two are often intertwined, but it is possible and helpful to explore their differences.

Tangible Goals

Tangible goals often support intangible goals. For example, life-expectancy in the United States is directly correlated with income. Obviously, being better-off does not directly improve one's health, but being able to get better quality medical care does. In a material world, the intangibles come easier when the economic basics are taken care of.

Surprisingly enough, it's not hard to teach people how to make more money. Studies have demonstrated that attaining economic security is actually an "entrance goal"—a gate which offers access to the rewards beyond it. Only after people overcome their fear of not having enough money do they begin to work in earnest on health, relationships, children, and personal satisfaction.

Intangible Goals

Most people's intangible goals relate to their family life. While people often initially focus their goals on improving their work and their incomes, the pleasures at work are limited unless life is good at home. Many people talk about their work as if it were central, but long-term goals are rarely limited to work-related activities.

Health, like family, is another major area of goals. How you perceive your responsibility for maintaining your health says much about your attitudes and your lifestyle. Every doctor knows a few patients who recover from a serious condition despite a negative prognosis. Many long-term ailments have been turned around when aided by careful and consistent goal setting.

A special health-related concern is overweight. The goal, thought through, is not merely to lose weight; it is to develop a self-concept which includes sufficient self-control as well as the capacity to maintain a healthy, physically appealing weight.

Other goals include learning new skills or upgrading old ones. These range from overcoming academic "weaknesses" in math or writing to learning new technologies, from improving one's golf, tennis, or skiing to learning new languages. To be able to learn whatever you wish, without anxiety, allows you to anticipate and bring to pass those changes which can enhance your future. As lifelong learning becomes more and more of a necessity, many people set, as a goal, improving their capacity to remain effective students.

Individual goals may strengthen character, especially when they include being comfortable in groups, managing time more effectively, or being kinder, more understanding or more confident. For example, a successful financial analyst I know used to sit through endless presentations about new ventures, real estate partnerships, and other investments, often wishing that he could be as self-assured and as interesting as some of the speakers. Ultimately, he set a goal; he decided to become, himself, a speaker in high demand, whose presentation was so stirring that he would receive a standing ovation whenever he spoke. Seven years after he started toward this goal, he was giving thirty talks a year (and turning down an equal number), most of which ended with a standing ovation.

CHOOSING AND DEVELOPING GOALS

The very act of setting goals affects your future. Before you begin to work toward a goal, you need to be sure that you desire it right now, and to be as sure as you can that achieving this particular goal will bring contentment. Let us look at some critical questions that can facilitate the process.

Question 1:
Do I Truly Want What I'm Asking For?

How much of your present life is as you desire it? How many hours of your day are as you desire them? Are too many of your activities performed primarily to please or placate others? Is some of what you do just to get by or to serve the goals of others? The following could help you ferret out those parts of your life that are less than they could be. It may be a disconcerting exercise, but for many people it has proved to be a useful one.

> When you awake in the morning, do you really *want* to get up? Really think about it!
> You take your bath or shower. Do you do it because you like it? Is it something you look forward to?
> What about your breakfast? Is it exactly the breakfast you like, in kind and quantity? Is it *your* breakfast you eat, or simply "breakfast" as defined by society? Do you, in fact, want it at all?
> As you go through your day, ask yourself: Have I freely chosen to be where I am and to be doing what I'm doing? Am I talking to people the way I want to? Do I really like or only pretend to like people I'm dealing with?
> Spend the whole day asking questions—*do I really like this or that?* As evening approaches ask yourself: What would I truly like to do? Am I doing it?
>
> (Adapted From Orage, *ON LOVING,* 1965)

It's important to know *what* you like. The *doing* of what you like comes later. The most unfortunate people I know are those who worked to achieve goals that were *not really theirs*, so that each achievement, reached through determination and effort, felt false, and each triumph was a hollow one. Striving for something you've talked yourself into is like running well, as fast as you can—but in the wrong direction.

Question 2:
Can I Express My Goal Clearly—In Writing?

All too many of us have goals which are vague and nebulous:

"I want to be happy."

"I want to be successful."

"I wish things would get better."

"I want to be in a good relationship."

These are goals and they sound positive, but they are so general that they don't offer a clue how or where to start. To wish for happiness is indeed a positive idea, but it pretty well leaves you where you started. The more precise the goal, the more easily it can be achieved. "I want to spend more time with my oldest daughter; to meet my sales quota without being overworked, to stop being afraid when I drive over bridges, and to control my arthritis so I can play tennis again." With statements like these, you at least know where to start.

Clear written goals are important for another, less obvious, reason. Each of us is many people—a parent, a worker, a lover, a liar, an athlete, a lazybones, a spendthrift, a miser. These inner people are in constant debate, polling their varied attitudes toward our actions. Each aspect of our personality has its own agenda.

In writing down a goal, we're allowing it to be reviewed by this internal "committee," to determine how many members really want it. If the answer is "most of them," it is a goal that can be achieved more quickly than one which is buffeted about by inner bickering. For example, I go to bed and my "hard worker" says, "Tomorrow I'll get up a half-hour early, do some exercise, write those two troubling personal letters, eat a really good breakfast, finish weeding under the plum tree, and call my editor in Berkeley. Then I'll get on with my day." How splendid, I think. What planning! What good sense! I slip into sleep smiling. The next morning, however, is dark and cold. I reluctantly recall my noble ideas of the previous night, but the lazy part of me is snug and warm in bed: "A little extra sleep and I'll feel better." As I turn over, I wonder, sleepily, who it was that decided to do all that extra work. I wish him well.

Write out what matters to you; in this way, your "committee" can review, study, modify, approve, and then *support your getting it.*

Question 3: Should I Set Time Limits?

If doubling your income is your goal, do you really want to wait several years or would you accept it sooner? If your blood pressure is too high, is lowering it something you want to put off till a better time? If you crave more time to travel, how long would it please you to postpone the realization of that goal?

The business community uses progress charts, five-year plans, quarterly goals, and so on as planning tools, because they let managers perceive future goals and make "guestimates" of how long things should take. Is it all right to scrap these timelines as the situation changes? Of course it is, how else would a company adapt to a changing market place. The need both to set and to change time limits would seem good common sense.

But both my observations and my experience suggests something other than the conventional wisdom, and something beyond dozens of otherwise adequate systems taught to managers, and educators. It is actually faster, and easier, and more in tune with the natural rhythms of the world, *not* to establish target dates for your goals. Your goals are what you want *right now;* setting time limits actually pushes achievements off into the future. A corporation president I worked with was extremely proud of his long-range plans. He had made a projection fifteen years ago that he'd double his company's revenues in five years, and he'd succeeded. At that point he'd made a new plan to again double in five years. Once again he succeeded. The third time he set the goal of doubling in five years, and was just as successful. He was content.

I asked him, "Would you be open to doubling your company in less than five years?" After weeks of discussions, he decided to leave his goals as they were, but to abolish his target times. A year passed. One day he phoned and said, "After working with you, the world seems much less stable. A number of things happened in our market which our last plan never anticipated. My managers felt freer to move quickly and they did. We've doubled in the last year, and scrapped the original plan. I still like the way I used to work, but it's foolish to deny superior results. Thanks for letting me out of my time limits!"

Don't set time limits. If you must, do it with your eyes open so that you don't confuse what you expect with what is actually possible. Goal-setting is a game; the advantage of working without time limits is that you get to win more quickly and more often.

Question 4: Should I Set Goals for Others?

Wouldn't it be wonderful if the neighborhood bully reformed, your alcoholic neighbor stopped drinking and the kids on the other side of you started playing soft classical music? It makes more sense, though, to develop ourselves so that we no longer attract nor fear that bully, are angry at our neighbor, are disturbed by the kids. It's harder by far to change others than to improve ourselves. We have neither the permission nor the tools to set goals for others. Hoping that someone else will change is a lazy way to improve one's life.

Lurking in the wish to change others is the shadow of a low self-concept as well as the belief that the outer world controls and determines our happiness. The external world offers us sunshine and rain, full stomachs and empty ones, successes and mistakes. But it does not rule us. How we use what we are given is inside us. Other people do not create our inner world; *changing other people will not change our inner world.*

All this notwithstanding, there are times when it makes sense to set goals for others. If you're a supervisor, your job is to help your people to be productive and successful. Goal-defining clarifies the job, and helps people make the most of their opportunities. But, in general, the less you intrude on others' goals, the more likely they are to set their own. People thrive when they know they are free.

Most people understand that setting goals for others is not appropriate, but still they pressure their spouses or children. They say, "Well... this is different. I know him or her as well as I know myself! I know what changes would make him or her happy." I am chilled by such remarks. Although they arise from loving concern, they contain the underlying assumption: "I am better qualified to run your life than you are."

My father hoped for years that I would get a regular job—a single employer, security, benefits, stability, and a clear career path. He didn't push his position and what he envisioned for me didn't happen. I managed to be productive—but in a variety of jobs—juggling and meeting my various responsibilities. As I became more successful, it became evident to my father that my family had neither suffered nor starved in the process. He had so wished to set that goal for me—for my own good, and for his peace of mind. Yet he refrained, and we both benefited profoundly.

A marriage truly is liberating and supportive when each partner esteems the other so completely that neither set goals for the other. Each spouse respects and enjoys the other's changes; each enjoys what the other achieves. Each appreciates a spouse who has the confidence and ability to make their decisions.

Question 5: Are My Goals Realistic?

Goals must make sense in terms of one's current life—they must be goals *you* can imagine. I have worked with people whose set goals were to have a net worth of ten million dollars and more—they achieved those goals. For those people such goals were realistic. Your goals must be based on your ideas of what is currently possible. What is eventually possible may be something else. Keep it realistic, but keep it moving—a good slogan for goal getters. As you succeed, move your goal up. As your life expands, don't be frozen by prior preset limits.

I collect stories which help me discern when my thinking or my beliefs may hamstring my efforts—where I need to expand my vision of the possible. Here are two from my collection.

I

Tim Agerter is a nineteen-year-old from Munster, Indiana. In pre-game warm-ups before Ohio State football games, Tim breaks down field, cuts and leaps high to haul in a pass. He takes a center snap, drops back and throws a pass. Once in a while he lofts a short spiraling punt. What sets the fans buzzing is that Tim does it all on one leg. His right leg was amputated at age three. He sees nothing unusual about the speed, agility, and balance he displays. In high school he was a competitive wrestler and high jumper. As a 105-pound wrestler, he reached the state semi-finals and as a high jumper cleared 6 ′4 ″. He continues to make the most of his abilities.

(condensed from a newspaper article)

II

Ivor Welsh runs marathons. He takes six hours or more to finish the twenty-six miles, but he finishes. He was eighty-five when he ran his first marathon, Before I heard of Ivor, I would have considered what he did impossible. Ivor didn't even start serious running until he was eighty-two; another fuse in my mind melted when I learned that. After hearing a talk of Ivor's, I asked him about his goals. His eyes lit up; he was thinking of doing the Pike's Peak Marathon next year. He was electric—excited, and filled with a joyful appreciation of his opportunities. Months later, I opened a newsletter from a runner's club. On the cover was a picture of Ivor, smiling and wearing a Pike's Peak Marathon T-shirt.

There are ways to move toward your goals—ways which work. It is vital to really know what you want, to be explicit about it, to be realistic, and to start *now*. The next step is to understand the impact of parts of your past, then to see how to change the unsatisying patterns. There is no need to settle for less than you really want or less than you can do.

II

SELF-CONCEPT

▲▲

The greatest revolution in our generation
is the discovery that human beings,
by changing the inner attitudes of their minds
can change the outer aspects of their lives.
—WILLIAM JAMES

If you don't start, you can't play.
If you don't play, you can't win.

Setting goals may be a simple matter; but it is only a first step. You encounter powerful forces when you perceive and confront the obstacles standing between you and your goals. Identifying these obstacles is only the beginning of the process. Merely understanding the pitfalls is insufficient; you need to learn how to overcome problems to make goals become truly achievable. One travels the route between wishful thinking and realizing goals through an artful combination of knowledge and effort.

BASIC ASSUMPTIONS

The more we learn about our natural tendencies,
the easier it is to teach ourselves how to be good,
how to be happy, how to be fruitful,
how to respect ourselves, and how to love.

—ABRAHAM MASLOW

We all have immense potential, and possess gifts which are undeveloped and therefore unavailable. Unsure of our upper limits, most of us settle for less than we are, letting opportunities pass by, unable to reach out to take what might be ours.

Biologists know that what is true for *one* member of a species is potentially true for *any* member of that species. If there is one white crow, more white crows are possible; if one redwood tree is 250 feet high and thirty feet around, other redwoods can grow that tall and that massive. Anyone with a special gift or capability is a living indication that the same potential exists in each of us.

The popularity of long-distance running in the 1980s made it clear that almost anyone willing to train properly could run long distances. Small miracles abound in the literature: people over eighty years old finish marathons; a fifty-four-year-old woman vies for a place on the U.S. Olympic women's marathon team against others half her age; people run across the entire country. Given a believable hope and the right support, we can vastly improve our condition and capacity, as well as transcend our previous expectations.

Studies of unusual people is a reminder that what are assumed to be natural limits do not inhibit people whose goals exceed them. I think of my memory, for example, as fairly good within "natural limits." But was Arturo Toscanini's memory, which enabled him to conduct entire symphonies without a score, unnatural? Was the memory of the politician James

Farley unnatural because he could recognize, by face or name, over 20,000 people? Have I accepted a limit for my memory well below my potential capacity?

When I fumble over my checkbook or become confused doing my tax return, I may console myself with the idea that "I'm just not good with numbers." Yet Nicholas Birns, at five years of age, amused and amazed adults by telling them what day of the week any date fell upon. Squirming and giggling, he would announce that April 12, 1947, had been a Wednesday while October 21, 1929, had fallen on a Monday. He was right, of course, but didn't know how he knew. Who knows his or her true potential?

I knew a reporter for the *New York Times* who could recall almost everything he had ever read. Asked to remember a poem or a quotation, he'd close his eyes and would begin to recite the passage. How did he do it? "I see the pages in my mind," he said. "When I was a kid, I thought everybody could do it. I thought that's why people were so excited when they learned to read."

The facts are inescapable: our species has vast potential. To realize that neither collectively nor individually have we reached our true limits is a first step. We need to confront the parts of ourselves that create unnecessary limitations and go on to overcome them!

The Nature of the Self-Concept

To know what you can become, you must first know who you are. Most of us do have a partial idea; we know our names, our sex, our nationality, our education, our skills, and our family history. We have memories of our childhood, our schooling, and places where we've lived. We know how we tend to act and what we have done. We know what we won't do, (or can't do) or at least haven't done until now. If we compare ourselves with others, we are better than or worse than someone else in this and that area.

Self-concept is the governing element of inner life. It is the sum of these many individual judgment calls; it is our actual evaluation or opinion of ourselves, and it determines how slowly or quickly we will achieve our goals, if at all. A high self-concept is expansive—supporting us in new ventures, learning new skills, and setting new goals. A low self-concept is restrictive—preventing us from trying new ventures ("I'll fail"), learning new skills ("I'm not smart enough"), or achieving new goals (I can't get what I want").

The good news is that everyone has considerable untapped potential. Each of us, however, also has a self-concept that reinforces our sense of our personal limitations.

Your personal effectiveness is exactly equal to your current self-concept. You have become no more than you imagine yourself able to be. And it follows that your opinion of yourself will be accurately reflected in the level of your accomplishments.

What arises from this assumption is the idea that if we can in some way raise self-concept, the level of achievements will rise as well. Our internal portrait and our external effectiveness will both increase.

Self-concept is a key to our future—more important than family connections or educational opportunities, and quite possibly the factor that determines our ultimate personal health and physical well-being. Just as important, self-concept is *learned*. Built up over time, it resists change, but *it can be changed effectively*.

THE STRUCTURE OF THE MIND

The mind is like a deep well; very little of it is "visible." The portion which is, we call consciousness. While it is a tiny amount of the whole mind, it includes everything that we are aware of at any given moment. We learn, consciously, in school; we act, consciously, at work; many of the feelings and experiences of daily life in our relationships are conscious ones.

Deeper down in the mind is the subconscious. Much vaster in extent, it contains memories—a complete detailed record of past experiences. It records and stores our opinions and our feelings about other times and places. The subconscious is not dormant, nor passive; it directly and continuously affects conscious processes, in part by supplying or withholding memories and feelings and in part by urging and demanding actions not fully understood by the conscious part of the mind.

How often have you said to yourself: "Why did I say that?" "What is so upsetting about this?" "What does that remind me of?" While we like to believe that we act consciously, many actions originate directly from the subconscious, completely bypassing the filter of our consciousness. You can, sometimes, drive for miles with almost no recall of what you passed or how you drove. To call someone "absent-minded" is only to observe a time when their conscious was not involved in the moment-to-moment details of their daily life.

Sigmund Freud concluded that no mental process occurs randomly. There is a cause for every thought, feeling, memory, or action. If "I" am not "aware" of the cause, this means only that my conscious mind is unaware.

How does the subconscious function? We know it stores the details of experience; it ensures, in many ways, that our actions are consistent with our ideas about ourselves. We never rush to the mirror in the morning and wonder who is there, no matter how tired or bleary an image confronts us. We are never, in fact, without a sense of identity. So strong is this subconscious portrait that when we act in an unusual manner, we remark on the strangeness:

"Something must have gotten into me to behave like that."

"I'm just not that way."

"I never do that kind of thing."

It unsettles our conscious opinion of ourselves when we behave out of character, but we do. So life becomes, among many other things, an endless quest to bring to light the hidden habits, motives, urges, and memories that lead us to do things which, at first blush, do not square with our self-concept.

Where then does self-concept reside? It includes the conscious summation of a great many attitudes. But, like an iceberg, most of it is hidden from awareness and resides in the subconscious.

FORMING OUR SELF-CONCEPT

At birth, we are pure potential. We have not learned any "limitations." The early years of childhood are times of exceptional growth, for to the unstructured mind everything seems possible. There is no other period in which we learn so quickly and so easily. Children learn consciously at first; then gradually turn learning into habits.

In learning to walk, we first toddle, paying attention to each step. Should we be distracted—flop! . . . down we go onto our diapered bottoms. Eventually walking becomes second nature. and we can turn our attention to other things, such as what to head for and why.

The development of habits streamlines the learning process and gives one the ability to learn more. William James, the first great American psychologist, wrote in 1890: "Habit is the enormous flywheel of society, its most precious conservative agent. . . . The more of the details of our daily life we can hand over to the effortless custody of habits, the more our higher power of mind will be set free for their own proper work."

Habits that permit effortless activities, such as walking, talking and reading are external expressions of mental structures. To walk, a child needs not only the necessary maturity and practice, but also a structure to generate inner statements such as "I want to walk . . . I can walk . . . I am a person who walks." Each of these statements becomes part of a growing self-concept. "I want . . ." orients the conscious mind. "I can . . ." reinforces the natural capacity to achieve. "I am. . ." is a recognition of actual and anticipated achievements.

Habits critical to self-concept development are taught in early childhood just as language is—by hearing the same message over and over again. While habits are valuable and necessary, they can also diminish our capacities—lowering the amount of conscious attention we give to our actions. Habits that blind us prevent further learning. We see it in children as they listen, understand, and accept parental guidance while learning early habits. Most eventually shift from constant discovery to an occasional revelation, a momentary insight. They lose the delight and wonder of seeing things freshly; they learn how everyone else sees and understands things. They stop saying and imagining the unexpected and begin to reflect what others have said and thought. They learn their family's habits of thinking, feeling, and acting which make it easier to get along. They learn how to survive—at a price.

When your parents told you, "You're a good child," it was not altogether clear what they meant by it. Slowly, through experience, you discovered which activities were "good"—saying please or sharing a toy. Squeezing the cat too hard was *not* good, nor was dumping your milk on your sister. More and more you began to act in accordance with what you'd been told about yourself. In new situations you tried to be "good," as an experiment, to see if it paid off. If it led to approval, love, and support, you tended to do it next time. If it did not, you tried something else.

Our self-concept is created primarily through the ways we devise to gain the love and support of our parents. To young children, parents are the most powerful forces in the universe; not only are they the major sources of love, security and information, but they are also the distributors of punishment and discipline. In short, the world of a child revolves around being on the favorable side of its parents. It is not simply that whatever parents say is right; it is far stronger than that. Whatever our parents tell us, when we are very small, has all the power and authority of God speaking to Moses. There are no safe alternatives to our parents' opinions. And so we develop a correct set of habits. But some of these are restrictive—they lower our opinion of ourselves, and worse, they stubbornly resist conscious modification.

Imagine you are three years old, sitting at the table with a small cup of milk. You move your hand excitedly; the cup tumbles to the floor. Plastic, it bounces once or twice before coming to rest amidst the blobs of milk. From your perch you enjoy the play of white against the colors of the floor. So far, no problem. But Mommy does not appreciate it. "You're so *clumsy!*" (Note this word.) "You clean up your mess!" Released from your chair, you clean up the milk. You toy with the new word "clumsy." What could it mean? The act of making splashes of milk? The next day, back in your chair with your lunch, you look at your half-filled glass of milk and decide to recreate your artistry. Over it goes. Once again your mother (no appreciation of art) growls at you. "I'm so tired of your clumsy behavior. Clean it up, all of it!" Again you mop up and again the inner considerations: "Clumsy . . . um, seems to be a trick I do with milk. Mommy doesn't like it."

A few days later, you spill your orange juice. Your mother asks your father, "Honey, will you clean it up? Jonathan is so clumsy." You hear what's being said about you. You think you understand. These acts of spilling are part of your character— part of the way you behave! Mom, who knows all things, has told you a terrible truth about yourself. *You are clumsy!* You are Jonathan Albert Dennison, you are three years old, you have a dog named Teddy and a teddy named Pup. You are a good boy; you are Mommy's little sweetie; you are Daddy's favorite fella. You know a lot about yourself, and now you are learning something new—*you are clumsy.*

It's no tragedy. It's just one more fact in your life, but once implanted, it grows until it is a critical part of your self-concept. It suggests how to think about yourself and how to behave.

Years later, in school, someone suggests forming clay on a wheel or climbing a rock. You consider it, and notice it clearly takes physical dexterity and skill. "No," you say, "I don't want to do that. It's not for me" Inside, part of you says, "I don't want to do that because *I am clumsy*, and I won't do it well."

In high school you're shy about dancing. "I don't like to dance" is the way you voice it, and you never learn to dance. Later you avoid skiing, windsurfing, or volleyball—any number of activities which call for overcoming the ineptitude of any beginner.

Parents, quite literally, do the best job they can. It was not your mother's intention to have you grow up clumsy, but your self-concept is built from what you're told or overhear and what your parents and others around you believe to be true.

Why do children accept these limitations?

It is crucial to grasp the power that parents wield in our early development; *their opinions have the force of facts*. If they are sorry that you're clumsy, that only makes it worse. If they could help you, they would—so your clumsiness must be carved in stone. Can you overcome it? Not easily, since at first, to overcome it would be make your parents wrong. To achieve your goals you need to become able to reverse and revise patterns deeply engraved into you by the most powerful people in the world. Remembering and understanding are the first steps.

III

LIMITATIONS

Those who believe that they can do
something
and those who believe they can't
are both right.
—HENRY FORD

We were born free but we find ourselves hemmed in by life's curious mix of obligations. We envy the careless abandon of small children as they fling themselves into one interest after another. Sadly we lack their easy flow from tears to laughter, from play to quiet, from chores to games.

There are all kinds of limitations in our personal life. There are physical laws which constrain us, as well as prohibitions—political, social and economic realities which restrict our choices. Yet the limitations that loom the largest are those we maintain on our own, portable cages, ready to drop over us to stop us when we could actually go ahead. Horses are not the only creatures wearing blinders to restrict their vision. We find ourselves willing, often determined, to maintain our blinders out of ignorance of our condition. As people come to recognize the origin of their limitations, they begin to take them off, to shake loose of inhibitions, compulsions, even phobias, placed on them in childhood.

INHIBITIONS

We start by looking at inhibitions, subtle self-imposed limits on intentions, feelings, thoughts, and actions. They prevent taking even the first step. They are DO NOT ENTER signs in front of unlocked doors.

At the root of all inhibitions, of course, is fear; yet to prevent experiencing fear, conscious reason rationalizes the inhibitions so it might appear beneficial. We speak of "limiting risks," "safeguarding against failure," not "losing time," or "being adult" about one's capacities. Sometimes these disguises fool us; sometimes—when the fear is more potent—they do not.

You can test this for yourself. Take a moment to complete these sentences. If any may make you uncomfortable, that's simply a reflection of the problems we all face when trying to perceive self-maintained barriers.

I can't _____

I have no aptitude for _____

I'm not able to _____

I've no skill at _____

I've never been able to _____

I'm no good in _____

I know better than to think I could _____

Now move on from this freshly created list of personal limits and consider another group of sentences, more positive and sensible-sounding, but just as chilling.

I'm just being realistic.

I'm nobody's fool.

We all have to accept our natural limitations.

Once bitten, twice shy.

You can't do everything you want.

You can't get blood from a stone.

Such statements are rattling around in our heads, ready to be used, when we are offered a new challenge, or encounter a novel situation. We all come to believe in, accept, and stay within the fence of our inhibitions. We don't call them fears, of course, instead we talk of "the natural maturing process" that occurs as wide-eyed children are turned into cautious and sensible adults.

As a boy, at summer camp in the mountains of Southern California, I played on large outcrops of huge granite boulders separated by crevasses that my friends and I leapt across. We called ourselves "The Mountain Goats," and assumed that our capacity to make long leaps was natural (and it was). Twenty years later, I visited the area, climbing on those same outcroppings, I was appalled at the risks that I'd once taken so casually.

The drops were thirty to fifty feet; the landing surfaces were jagged rocks. I could leap farther now, but I couldn't bring myself to make the same jumps. Call it good judgment or prudence if you like, but it felt like a limitation.

We all have some limitations which inhibit us. These are not trivial, nor are they illusions. They form part of our character, our personality, and our self-concept.

Can you overcome your unwillingness to brave a new situation? Can you overcome a fear of failure, based on actual failures suffered in the past?

Of course you can. The first step in regaining your freedom is to accurately describe your prison. Then you can begin to tunnel your way back to freedom.

COMPULSIONS

An inhibition is a DO NOT ENTER sign; a compulsion is a YOU MUST ENTER sign. Inhibitions prevent you from starting things; compulsions pressure you and leave you no choice.

Just as inhibitions can be ways to protect you from fear, compulsions are often artfully concealed as virtues. Consider neatness: it is useful to be neat. We can find our belongings; we don't create messes that might offend others, and so forth. However the virtue can have a compulsive shadow side: "I *must* keep my things neat and clean."

Why must you?

It may obviously be a better way to be, but that does not explain the compulsion. Underlying the "must" is the fear that if you don't keep everything in order, something bad will happen.

Suppose, for a moment, that you are a compulsively neat or tidy person, and that, due to illness or accident, you're unable to keep your world in order. Your home becomes dusty and cluttered. Mail lies unanswered, bills remain unpaid, phone messages are not returned.

When I've asked people to play out this fantasy, their discomfort level has sometimes risen to an intolerable level: they ask me to end the exercise. Occasionally, their anxiety resolves to a conscious fear of impending punishment, usually including a cloudy vision of a parent. Sometimes the fear breaks, erupting into laughter. When the vision of punishment is followed by a review—through adult eyes—of childhood conditioning, fear dissipates, and, instantly, the compulsion becomes more manageable.

Insight alone seldom fully overcomes a compulsion, but it opens the door to objective examination. Rabia, a colorful and perceptive saint, once prayed, "Lord, if I serve Thee in hope of Heaven, send me to Hell. If I serve Thee in fear of Hell, send me to Hell. I would learn to serve Thee for love of Thee and love alone." She understood the limitations bred by fear as well as the masks it maintains—compulsions and inhibitions.

If you're open to uncovering some of your own compulsions, one way is to complete the following sentences:

I have to _____

I must _____

Everyone should _____

Why don't people all _____

We become compulsive to escape anxiety. We learned that it was worth the extra time it took, as well as any inconvenience to ourselves or others, to feel less fear. As adults we continue to act out concerns implanted during childhood. Once we had to be on time to avoid a spanking, now we are on time "so that we won't hold up other people," or "just out of common courtesy." The conscious reasons have changed, but not the behavior.

RESTRICTIVE HABIT PATTERNS

Inhibitions and compulsions are two examples of what are called restrictive habit patterns. These habits have a number of aspects:

- They restrict freedom of choice and action.

- They are implanted during childhood and are linked to fear.

- They are largely unconscious.

A restrictive habit pattern is beyond your conscious control. *It behaves you.* Once triggered, it demands that you act or not act in a set fashion, and once set into motion, it is difficult to stop or modify.

One vivid restrictive habit pattern is a phobia—a fear so disproportionate to the situation that the frightened person even acknowledges its irrational dimensions. Spiders are small, ninety-nine percent harmless, and most people are not afraid of them. But if you have a phobia about spiders, and you see a spider, all that good sense vanishes: all you know is that *you must get away.* Psychological methods to treat phobias usually help people to look beyond the immediate fear reaction to the childhood pattern in which the fear is embedded.

In childhood we all learned how to best hold the love and attention of our parents, how also to avoid pain, discomfort, loss of love, and fear. Those protective habits were the best solutions available to us at the time; however, retaining them as adults has a price—the artificial restriction of our freedom and the damping down of our own capabilities. If we could, we'd release these childhood patterns when the need for them passed. But since they are repressed out of awareness, we cannot see them. *The causes, the origins, are no longer remembered.* Fear is especially devastating to a child so that ''How I can avoid fear and how do I avoid pain?'' become daily questions very early in life. We learn to take any action which will take us out of range, and away from danger.

Consciously, we learn not to approach or do anything that will increase our fear. Subconsciously, we take a more subtle and perplexing step. We try to avoid letting the conscious part of our mind even notice the threat. We turn the avoidance, the flight from fear, into an automatic reaction—so well structured that it does not need conscious attention. Just as we move our fingers off a hot stove without having to think about it, our habit patterns run us without conscious help or awareness. If we can avoid being afraid without noticing, so much the better.

A friend of mine who enjoyed learning piano was hurt, in childhood, when his parents announced to friends that he had no special talent for music. He soon stopped playing the piano. Hearing his own playing recalled his parents' negative opinion and the resulting fear that they would love him less. He was less unhappy if he did not play. And so, no more playing and no more fear, but no more piano. As an adult not only did he not play an instrument, but when he entered a living room with a piano, he sat as far away from it as possible. These were not conscious actions but were the progressive refinement of the initial restrictive habit pattern, to avoid fear restimulated by seeing a piano. When he was asked to observe his own behavior, it came as a complete surprise to him—until he was helped to recall how it had started. He had continued to love music, but after finally being able to face his subconscious need to escape from parental disapproval, he decided to overcome his phobia—not by forcing himself to play the piano, but by learning and becoming proficient on a different instrument.

MISTAKES—CRITICISM—GUILT

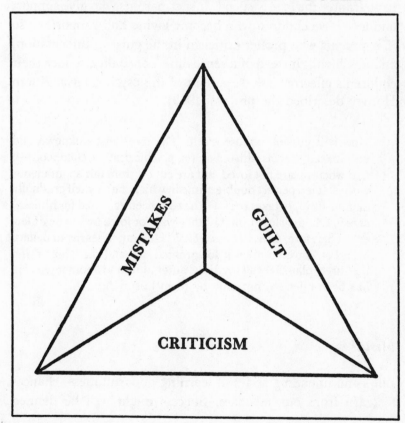

Consider the preceeding diagram—a pyramid in which each side reinforces the others. Mistakes, criticism, and guilt combine and interact to restrict personal happiness.

How do we acquire the burden of mistakes, the belittling effects of criticism, the stinging scars of guilt? We are brought up exposed to the expectations and opinions of our parents which can become self-fulfilling prophecies. What we are told about ourselves often comes unerringly to pass. If we're told that it's shameful of us to think, or act, a particular way, we will feel shamed when we are that way, or when we think about being that way. Then, to protect ourselves, we will strive to repress those aspects of ourselves and they persist.

We may resist; we may became defiant. We may even use the force of parental disapproval to forge a powerful and independent identity. But more often we capitulate, to feel secure and to guarantee the love we need. Just as parents who give support and love have children who become loving and supportive, so may parents who proffer criticism in the guise of information, and instill guilt instead of a sense of responsibility, reduce their children's effectiveness. A patient of the psychoanalyst Karen Horney described the process (1949):

> How is it possible to lose a self? The treachery, unknown and unthinkable, begins with our secret, psychic death in childhood—if and when we are not loved and are cut off from our spontaneous wishes. It is a perfect double crime in which the tiny self gradually and unwittingly takes part. He has not been accepted for himself, *as he is.* Oh, they love him, but they want or force him to be different! Therefore, *he must be unacceptable.* He himself learns to believe it and at last even takes it for granted . . . and the whole thing is entirely plausible; all invisible, automatic, and anonymous. He has been rejected, not only by them but by himself.

Mistakes

Life is an unending series of learning opportunities—chances to learn from our mistakes. Success might well be defined as the highly developed ability to profit from errors and turn mistakes into useful experiences. The lives of the most celebrated successful people are peppered with stories of their fumblings and their recoveries, *and how they learned from them.* Entrepreneurs average about four failures to each major success. What distinguishes truly successful human beings is their unwavering sense of self-worth. All of us are continually testing out a behavior or an idea. Should it succeed, we are likely to try it again; if it fails, we either learn from the failure and try a different activity, or *not* learn, resistant or oblivious or both, and make the mistake again. If we repeat an unsuccessful response often enough, it may become a restrictive habit pattern; both the event and its results can get blocked out of awareness. Parents who say, "If I've told you once, I've told you a thousand times" are parents who've found a way that doesn't work and stayed with it. Stuck at the end of a blind alley, they are unable or unwilling to learn a more effective approach.

A common cause of mistakes is a simple lack of information. If you don't know that today is a bank holiday and go to cash a check, you'll have made a mistake. If you are learning a different word-processing program and lose an important file, you probably made a error in typing the commands. Next time you'll review the manual. You gossip to someone about a third party; later you find out the two are old friends. We've all had to pay for, and hopefully learn from, our ignorance.

Mistakes may also arise from restrictive habit patterns in areas beyond your control and sometimes outside of awareness. During a job interview, the interviewer lights a cigarette—and you happen to dislike smoking intensely. You might become rattled and lose track of what is being said. The remainder of the interview doesn't go well. Strictly speaking, the fault is not yours since you are not aware of the extent of your reaction nor its impact on the rest of your behavior.

Some people are labeled "accident prone." Objects fall from their hands or break at their touch; things just . . . happen to them. A few may have neurological problems, but most have a self-concept that includes the conviction that, "I'm just a clumsy person. I've always been clumsy. My folks always said that I found accidents just waiting to happen. I guess it's true. I don't pay attention around stuff.''

Patterns of mistakes that remain unchanged by new information are restrictive habit patterns. Take apologies. When people say, ''I just don't know what got into me,'' you're hearing an involuntary admission of a restrictive habit pattern. Truly unaware of their behavior, they limit their capacity to observe it and change it.

Mistakes happen because we don't know the right way or the right answer. If we've never learned, should we be punished or blamed? The world can treat mistakes harshly. It doesn't know or care that some of our mistakes are restrictive habit patterns— mechanical behaviors not open to consciousness. We should not blame ourselves for these, any more than we are apt to blame ourselves for our height or hair color. Friends, enemies, and, most amazingly, we ourselves, hold up our mistakes and demand that we feel shame, guilt, regret and remorse over these natural and inescapable events in our lives. From our earliest years, we've all shouted, ''It's not my fault!'' pleading to be liberated from the stinging nettles of *criticism*, the second side of the pyramid.

Criticism

The word ''critic'' derives from a Greek word meaning to discern or to see clearly. A more constricted meaning refers to someone who observes flaws or defects. Professional critics and reviewers are supposed to balance their observations and judgments, but they often damn more skillfully than they praise.

When criticism is objective, it can be helpful. Objective, informative criticism can lead to improved performance, greater safety, and better skills. When criticism is subjective—fault-finding without suggesting acceptable or useful ways of overcoming the error—we feel it as a direct and personal attack. Such criticism actually reduces subsequent effectiveness by diminishing self-concept.

Treating people as if they are incapable of learning to correct their mistakes eventually impacts their competence. There is a style of management which assumes that supervisors have to be hard on their staff, keep them in line, and chew people out when they foul up. Thank goodness, this approach is losing credibility and is rarely observed in companies which are growing, profitable, or innovative. It is a low self-concept style.

There is no situation, no matter how crucial, in which people will not make mistakes. When we are aided by informed, compassionate criticism we can learn. If the criticism is meant to hurt us, or glorify the critic, or if it fails to include corrective information, we will not learn and not improve. To be told that "You have mush for brains," or that "You are one stupid S.O.B." does not serve you, nor does it clarify the problem, and so doesn't improve your chances of doing better next time.

When children are called "stupid," "mean," "selfish," "irritating," "unkind," "ugly," "dumb'—their self-concept is damaged, and their capacity is diminished. When adults call each other these same names, the impact may be less, but the potential to be wounded is still there. There is no evidence that abusive criticism helps anyone.

Most of what we call criticism is not beneficial. On the contrary, it simply reinforces the tendencies which led to the initial criticism. People may improve their performance for a short time, out of fear, but long-term improvement comes from constructive, supportive advice, not from intimidation. In addition, abusive criticism harms the giver as well; it reinforces a pattern of hurting others.

Guilt

The wrong kind of criticism often engenders guilt, the third side of the pyramid. Guilt comes from the Anglo-Saxon word "gylt" for sin or crime. On the surface, it has two functions, both of them questionable.

First, guilt is used to control others. As Voltaire said, "If I can make a man feel guilty, I can control him." Second, guilt is used to punish. Guilt creates inner wounds not easily healed and causes suffering long after the event. In spite of the apparent effectiveness of guilt to control and punish, a closer examination reveals severe limitations.

Guilt does not lead to control. Voltaire was wrong. Guilt actually gives us permission and encouragement to commit the same "crime" again. When we say someone is guilty of doing such and such, we are labeling him or her as the kind of person who commits such acts. "I am a sinner" is a self-concept that can be maintained only by repeated sins. Thus the sins become permissible, since they are made part of one's self-concept. ("What can I do? That's the way I am.") Guilt, in fact, encourages the repetition of the act. Feeling guilty is a punishment, and experiencing and absorbing a punishment allows a person to feel that they have paid for their prior acts. Thus they can commit the act again, should the temptation recur.

Guilt persists. The experience of guilt somehow scars the mind. Most of us carry such scars acquired in childhood from well-meaning but overly critical parents, teachers, priests, and others, were scarred again as teenagers often in our relationships, and we continue to be scarred as adults by those who attempt to use guilt to manipulate us.

Guilt belittles. It makes us ashamed of some aspect of our lives. Guilt compounds a mistake, a single event, and labels it a character flaw—a defective building block in the foundation of our psyche.

Guilt spreads. People driven by guilt may let it leak from one area of their lives to another until they are hobbled with an ongoing vague sense of being to blame; then the taste of many daily experiences becomes polluted by guilt. People who complain that what they do is never good enough, that they never meet their goals, that they are always a disappointment to those around them, may be reflecting this vague sense of underlying guilt.

There are no benefits to giving or having guilt. There is no evidence that children who experience excessive guilt become better human beings. Erasing guilt is one of the great gifts that people can give to themselves or to one another. While the scars may not ever vanish, they can fade.

Mistakes lead to criticism, criticism to guilt, guilt to lowered overall effectiveness and so to new mistakes. Mistakes, in turn, create more criticism, and round and round it goes. Any effective work on yourself, therefore, must take into account the interactions among mistakes, criticism, and guilt. The vital question is how to break this cycle and open yourself up to lasting transformation.

THE POWER OF HABITS

To use habits well is part of living well. If a habit propels us in the direction we wish to go, it is invaluable. For example, driving a car is a complicated series of actions which, for most of us, has become a set of subconscious habits. By turning driving over to the subconscious, we are freer to use driving time for reflection, conversation, or sightseeing. If we change to a different car, we may become conscious of our driving habits for a few minutes while we rearrange our habits to fit the new car. Then off we go again, letting our habits do the driving. If the road conditions change from dry to icy, initially we pay closer conscious attention to the new situation, changing our habits to allow for it. Habit patterns can be modified by:

motivation

awareness

knowledge

practice

A liberating habit pattern, conscious and under your control, can displace a restrictive one. Making maximum use of consciously maintained habits is one of the ways to increase freedom and success. Adults can create, change, or extinguish prior habits. As children we had little control over the formation or elimination of habits; this aspect of our inner and outer lives was dominated by our parents and our own desire to please them and thus gain or retain their love.

To modify a positive useful habit is not difficult; all of the information is available to consciousness. To change a restrictive habit pattern is a subtler and more difficult problem. The reasons for the habit—the actual root causes—are often repressed and forgotten. The conscious mind may not even be aware of the habit. Restrictive habits inhibit new learning—adapting, growing and changing to fit new circumstances. Effective personal growth depends on gaining increased control over our habits.

BELIEVING IN LIMITS

A person is limited by what he
can hold in his imagination.
—WILLIAM JAMES

What are the limits of human ability? We have no real idea. Few of us reach our limits. The *Guinness Book of Records* is an ongoing compilation of the possible. Every page describes an upper edge of human functioning. Each new edition lists hundreds of prior records broken and hundreds of new ones created. What is striking is not the records themselves; it is the *changing records*—the continual surpassing, the pushing of the limits further and further. Each is a baseline for the next record-breaker. It is a book of limits asking to be exceeded!

In my neighborhood the high school track coach runs on his birthday. Every year his gift to himself is to run a mile for each year of his life. Last year, in his mid-forties, he ran an extra mile. "An extra candle," says he. At what age might he be unable to meet his commitment to himself? We cannot say.

Consider Bill Emmerton, probably the foremost long distance runner of our times. When he was fifty he ran 1100 miles in twenty-eight days. What are our limits?

The truth is that if we have the correct information and we have the will, some of our capabilities are almost limitless. One way to extend our ideas about our abilities and our limits is to learn how to develop and extend them. Instructors using accelerated learning techniques report that students often learn twice as much in half the time as with conventional methods. Much of the training had to do with unlearning previous limits.

Are there any limits? Of course; trees don't grow endlessly into the sky. But what is important to remember is that human achievement can reach staggering peaks. You don't have to to run twenty-six miles in a few hours to be in good health, but it's energizing, however, to realize that it's an achievable goal, one that already has been achieved by children under ten and adults over eighty-five.

If our goal is to be wealthy, it is not essential that we aim for a billion dollars. There are few billionaires, but there are dozens of millionaires in their early twenties in the United States alone, and many thousands of all ages worldwide. Some had advantages to start with but most had only information, a high self-concept and resolve. Similarly, if your goal is to have a happy marriage, it is yours to have once you learn how to grasp that goal. Our limits are within ourselves.

The opportunity to achieve high goals is a natural part of our legacy as human beings; it is given to us at birth. We have emphasized how it is that most of us use only a fraction of our latent capacities. Now let us begin to turn to see how we can overcome these limits.

IV

THE FORCES
OF
LIBERATION

▲▲

You are already enlightened,
the only question is:
how long will it take you
to realize this fact?
—KRISHNAMURTI

E very effective system of personal transformation identifies four steps which lead to increased health, fulfillment, and a more conscious productive life; the steps are motivation, awareness, knowledge, and practice.

MOTIVATION

We are all able to recognize our own discomfort, but whether we will begin to change is a different matter, even when we're able to identify the persistent habits which are at the core of

43

our problems. The first and most basic step toward overcoming such patterns to achieving a higher level of self-actualization is to develop sincere desire.

We all know people who say, in the face of reversals:

"It can't be helped."

"Other people have all the luck."

"Be grateful for small mercies."

"What can't be changed must be endured."

The implication, of course, is that while others might improve, not the speakers. Their self-concept does not permit them to see themselves as included among the more fortunate, the gifted, or the likely-to-be-rewarded. They haven't enough belief in themselves to begin to hope, thus the goals they might have set never are set and never are realized.

A first step—and it is only a first step—is to acknowledge that changing habit patterns seems to have been helpful for others and might be useful for you. But knowing this, by itself, is insufficient. Having acknowledged that you *want* to make your life work more effectively, you must immediately begin the second step— which is become more fully aware of the critical issues in your life.

AWARENESS

Awareness cures.

—TIM GALWAY

To be aware is to be able to observe what is true in your own life, what has happened to you in the past, and what you wish for your future.

As you become more aware, you will be able to notice those moments when you are not free. To the extent that you can see the effects of repression, limited self-concept, inhibitions and compulsions, timidity, awkwardness, lack of ambition, and lack of faith in yourself, you'll begin to overcome them.

There is a strange and delightful dance that consciousness does with awareness. Experience is the tiny portion of reality that you *notice*. Only with determined effort will you pay close attention to situations which make you uncomfortable. Unless you are motivated to change, you may live most of your life without exposing your weaknesses to the light. Once freed from whatever casts the shadow, you can clearly see parts of yourself that were hidden, and you can easily determine what needs to change.

The first moments of motivated awareness are a plunge into a cold, wave-battering ocean. The chill is intense—it lasts only a moment—and is soon forgotten in the pleasures you find as one opportunity follows another. There are waves asking to be ridden that you couldn't begin to see until you took that first bone-chilling dive. The pain of confronting opportunities passed by, of self-maintained anxieties, or of unsatisfying relationships— the half-conscious memories of how you may have hurt your children, lost chances to be truly happy, or allowed physical habits or excessive work to erode your health, begin to submerge in a cascade of new possibilities, suddenly perceived, and new strengths suddenly and clearly felt.

To stop at the brink of this new awareness is almost worse than not starting. To make a list of dreams that could be realized, of obligations to yourself that could be met, and then to put those visions aside again, creates more suffering than does ignoring them. Awareness is a magical tool for investigating your inner world to clarify what you would like to change. It must be followed by action, however, or you will find that the awareness fades again. Remaining aware, you can change any aspect of any habit that you choose. The choices and the decisions at last become yours.

KNOWLEDGE

*Those who have knowledge have responsibility, those
who do not have none.*
—IDRIES SHAH

**Once you know what you want, you then need to know how
to go about getting it.** There are mountains of self-help literature, seminars, tapes, classes and programs. They can be helpful, although most stop at the brink and skip a step. They increase
your motivation without giving you the tools necessary to do
the *preliminary work;* they talk about results before you have learned
enough to produce them. A continuous cycle of motivation, awareness, and know-how has to be established until a pattern that
can (and must) recur is developed. With each new step one
reevaluates motivations, refines awareness, and acquires current
and correct information.

The mere knowledge that we *can* grow is not enough; simply seeing that others have grown is not enough. It is understanding how they did it that becomes the vital link activating
the energy generated by desire and focused by awareness. Once
you understand the full range of what you can do for yourself
and acquire the knowledge you need, you create and control your
destiny.

Awareness without knowledge can bring on depression;
knowledge without action leads to frustration. Knowing which
tools you need to break out of your prison will not help you if
you have no hope of getting them. Having the tools at hand and
never using them may be even worse. Fortunately, once you know
the right thing to do, you will be drawn to do it. We have an
uncanny taste for the truths which liberate us. What you learn
along the way is that no person is ever finished; being truly alive
means to remain open to new possibilities and new responses.

You may well ask, "What then follows from knowledge?"
It's no mystery: after knowledge comes practice. Indeed, growth
comes to those who cultivate themselves.

PRACTICE

No one is so foolish that he does not desire wisdom.
Why then are we not all wise?
Because so much is required to that end.
—MEISTER ECKHART

The step from knowledge to practice is the last and most critical step in improving your life. Simply assuming responsibility does not seem to provide what it takes to leap over all hurdles between an original wish and the realized goal.

Perhaps the easy availability of facts has made us forget that knowledge is only an interim step. Knowledge without desire leads only to scholarship; knowledge without awareness leads only to egotism. Knowledge without practice leads to teaching others what you yourself do not do. Public officials tell us to be more thrifty with *our* funds while projects under their direction overrun the contracts by millions. The balding barber knows volumes about what you should buy to save your hair but not enough to save his own.

Moreover, when it comes to human development, much of what we call "knowledge" is only knowledge *about* a way of being, a condition, or a state of mind. It doesn't tell you how to get there or what to do about it; it only describes the thing from the outside. For example, I can see films or read about Paris; that is "knowledge about." But how to get to my hotel, where and what to eat, or what to do when the Metro closes, that is knowledge gained by direct experience. Knowledge *about* Paris is good, but knowing Paris is necessary if you ever plan to live there.

Calvin Coolidge, who, by legend, was the tersest of presidents, was asked after church one Sunday. "How was the sermon?"

"Good."

"What was it about?"

"Sin."

"What did he have to say about it?" asked the slightly exasperated questioner.

"He was against it," answered the president, terminating the discussion.

The prayer, "Lord, let me know my sins," is a good prayer; it is not, however, as useful as, "Lord, let me know what I may do to overcome my sins."

Knowledge is a stepping stone to action. The desire to become a fine diver we'll call the motivation. Awareness steers you to swimming pools with diving boards. Knowledge ensures that you will try to move your body correctly as you turn in the air. But only practice can make you a fine diver. Practice blends motivation, awareness, and knowledge into the heady experience we call success.

The basic business of living well comes from effective practice. Living a good life means being able to see oneself clearly—limitations as well as strengths. To live well means to use one's strengths correctly—skills acquired through determination and practice. It means having the understanding necessary to establish goals. It is knowing what you need, and being able to profit from your understanding.

We begin our lives in perfect freedom. But even childhood, thought of as a time of expansion, is a time when freedoms become limited. To push past these limitations, to take more and more responsibility for your own life, is what it means to become an adult This demands motivation, awareness, knowledge, and practice. We should never compromise in reaching for our freedom. When desire remains conscious, opportunities present themselves. We are never without sufficient tools for our own liberation.

V

RETRAINING
THE MIND

Most people live,
whether physically, intellectually or morally,
in a very restricted circle of their potential being.
We all have reservoirs of life to draw upon,
of which we do not dream.

—WILLIAM JAMES

We are often prisoners of what we think we know, unable to break out of self-generated errors. We act on our data as though it were true and real. The truth, of course, is that at times our information is incomplete, outdated, even incorrect. If we begin with false assumptions, the actions we take may well go wrong.

Can you recall a time when you overlooked the first day of Daylight Savings Time? You went to work an hour late, called someone an hour late, arrived somewhere an hour late. All of your good intentions, careful planning, scheduling and organizing could not alter or overcome your mistaken idea of what time it must be.

The problem is not that we lack the *capacity* to act differently; it is that false information prevents us from changing our behavior to our benefit. When we become aware that obsolete data left over from childhood restricts our freedom, we develop a desire to learn new, correct information. New data leads to new actions, which in turn can lead to new results.

REVISING OUR DATA

Is it difficult to revise assumptions about the world around us? No, we do it all the time. Our lives are a succession of opportunities to take in new information and so to think differently, plan differently, act differently.

In April of 1984, the San Francisco Bay Area was shaken by a long, moderately intense earthquake. Hundreds of people subsequently sought help and advice about earthquake protection, how to prepare for problems which could result from a stronger quake. People suddenly found it urgently necessary to know how to bolt their homes to the foundations, strap hot water heaters against the walls, store emergency food and water, and shut off gas and electricity.

What was the new data that sparked their interest? It was not that they learned that they lived in a major earthquake zone; of that they were already aware. It was the realization that they *personally* were living in such an area—that *their* house, *their* place of business, *their* children's school was at risk. Because of the recent quake, awareness was current and vivid. A year later, laws were changed which forced insurance companies to clarify, in large type, what kind of earthquake insurance was actually available. This was one response to these renewed personal concerns about earthquake preparedness. Another round of concern and fact-finding led to another law which forced insurance companies to offer such coverage to every homeowner in the area.

People are open to new, even if troubling, information which involves their welfare—*unless there are strong habit patterns which restrict awareness.* Smokers, for example, know about the health problems associated with smoking. Yet their habit is often too strong to allow real change. If you are *not* acting on current and valid information which could make you healthier, happier, or more effective, be assured that a restrictive habit pattern is running that portion of your life.

The process of changing concepts in the light of new information is almost universal. Years ago, one of my relatives came back from college declaring, "I want to buy shares of a company called Xerox." She had been to the university library, where for twenty-five cents she had made a copy of a single sheet of paper. Why buy Xerox? "Because," she said, "some day every university library in the country will want at least one of those machines." She was right, but her vision far smaller than the reality which followed.

Once an idea is unleashed, it has enormous power to affect our lives. The history of science is the history of one theory being accepted until new data contradicts it, forcing the birth of a new theory. There are bitter battles between proponents of the old theory and the champions of the new. Scientists are no different than the rest of us; their habit patterns sometimes obscure their perception of reality. Max Planck, Nobel Prize winning physicist, once said, "My theories will be accepted only after my colleagues are dead." Such rigidity by his professional colleagues seemed unlikely, but history proved him correct. Some part of us resists new data and clings to old habit patterns while other parts accept the new and actively seek out ways to change.

As we observed earlier, the effective development of new, more flexible habit patterns in our daily lives involves four steps:

motivation

awareness

knowledge

practice

These counterbalance the cycle of self-attack already described, consisting of:

mistakes

guilt

criticism

Since early childhood, success meant wanting something, learning how, and implementing what we have learned. A child has, first, a desire to walk. Then comes the learning, and finally the careful application of that learning into useful patterns.

But there is more to learning to walk than the learning itself; there is also the emotional effect of each step on the child's mind. The learning of something important includes the integration of each step along the way. As we learn new habits, the old ones, for better or worse, do not vanish from the mind. In learning to walk, we do not lose the capacity to crawl. Success is a heightened ability to transcend our past, making full use of those aspects still useful. Even more than our habits, our whole way of seeing and being in the world remains, neatly stacked, inside our minds. Should we need to recall, consciously or otherwise, any moment of the past, our early memories appear to be complete and in order. No one has a "poor memory." An inability to recall something simply means that we have not pierced the veil between the conscious and the subconscious. Changing ourselves is a matter, first, of understanding the habits we have developed and second, of no longer accepting the limitations to which we have become accustomed.

OVERCOMING BARRIERS
TO CHANGE

To what extent can motivated, knowledgeable people develop new habits?

I once counseled an overweight, belligerent, unemployed

young woman. She had used drugs for some years and had become phobic, unattractive, heavy, and sullen. She was too frightened to leave her house to go look for a job. She had no relationships. Extremely unhappy, she drank heavily, smoked and overate.

Because she valued the counseling sessions, I used them to motivate her. At her request we focused on her weight. I told her that she could see me each time she had lost three pounds. She wept and shouted, telling me I was unfair, that she was in counseling because she *couldn't* control her weight. I stood my ground.

She began to lose weight and her capacity to run her own life began to re-emerge. She put herself on an extremely strict, sound diet. Over the next few years, as the weight flowed off, she developed her own interests, took on a steady job, and eventually started her own business. The venture grew so rapidly that her husband (one other outcome of her improved self-concept) decided to leave his management position to work in her business. She taught me that *if you give a person who wants to change the information they need, the person will change.*

We do not know our limits. Consider smoking—a dominating, compelling, and addicting habit. When I teach I often ask if there are ex-smokers present and how they stopped. Usually more than half the group announce that they simply stopped smoking one day and never picked it up again. Hundreds of thousands of people have, the human spirit being what it is, by an act of personal courage and will, overcome serious addictions. There are numerous stop-smoking programs available and they work—when the smoker truly wants them to.

Alcoholics Anonymous has created a successful self-help program based on intention, information, and practice. The first step in their program is to acknowledge the problem and to be willing to accept help—people admit that they cannot control their drinking habits and that those habits are self-destructive. AA then provides information and support on how to change. They insist that the alcoholic who truly wishes to stop set a goal: to be sober "one day at a time." Each such day then becomes a day on which intention is reinforced, information is shown to be valid, and another successful day of sobriety gets completed. Each sober day makes the next one easier until, eventually, the practice becomes habit. People reaffirm their intentions through frequent meetings which stress that they are working at—and succeeding in—the creation of new habits. Meetings also always include a period of reminding members of their prior habits, and thus act to prevent new denial. Meetings of recovered drinkers emphasize the need to maintain the new habits and new goals.

In any situation, intention is limited only by what one believes. During a seminar I gave on goal setting, a slim and obviously healthy couple revealed that each had lost over thirty pounds in the last year, reversing years of weight gain. A class member asked about their diet. Both laughed, "We don't diet anymore . . . it never worked. Instead we came to realize that *we didn't have to be overweight.* Then we decided to go for the weight we wanted. Our meals came trailing after us, changing to meet our new demands." Their first step was information, the second was a changed intention; the results came from developing eating patterns that fit their new image of themselves.

A businessman wrote me a year after we'd worked together. His income had increased 700%. Putting to use what he'd learned, he had taken a careful look at his industry and observed that people working for large companies, as he was, had safe, stable jobs at about his salary level. But people who ran their own offices seemed to earn much more, though with occasional failures. He decided to take a risk—and freed from his prior limitations, he succeeded. Along with the higher income, he can now vary his hours to take extended vacations with his family.

A wise old man once described life as an obstacle course—a sequence of high and low hurdles, hedges, pits, and brick walls. In childhood, before we really start to run the course, we are fitted with blindfolds. Because we can't see very well, most of us slam into the obstacles, try to go around them, or tip them over. How much easier it becomes when we peek out from the blindfolds. Letting a limitation go drops a part of our blindfold.

What makes us sad and uncomfortable is the mistaken belief that our limitations are permanent:

"I'll *never* learn to swim/dance/bowl/skydive . . ."

"I'll *never* get a promotion/new job/loving spouse . . ."

If we don't get past that first feeling of discomfort, we'll never know if the obstacle was a mirage or a reality. When you don't play, you can't win.

We've seen how limitations are built into childhood, and that we save and store a complex maze of feelings, thoughts, memories and events. No single episode is separate from the whole. All thoughts, impulses, actions, and dreams are interconnected. It is a delightful and fascinating process to travel back down the inner pathways of one's past to try to identify those critical moments. You can, if you wish, search your early memories to discern root causes and uncover the origins of your patterns. To look into yourself is to discover a collection of personal treasures, for no one who deeply examines his or her own life can find it boring. However, exhuming your past is not as necessary as many people think.

You do not need to know the initial sources, from your childhood, in order to change. The first task is to identify the limitation as it affects you now—in the present. Childhood events are certainly pivotal, but are not the key to learning what to do to improve your life *now*. Carl Jung, the founder of analytical psychology, said it clearly:

> We seldom get rid of an evil by understanding its causes—and for all our insight, obstinate habits do not disappear until replaced by other habits. . . . No amount of confession and no amount of explaining can make the crooked plant grow straight; it must be trained upon the trellis . . .

THE PARADOX OF THE PRESENT

"Let everyone try, I will not say to arrest,
but to notice or attend to the present moment of time.
One of the most baffling experiences occurs. Where is it, this
present? It has melted in our grasp, fled ere we could touch it,
gone in the instant of becoming."
—WILLIAM JAMES

The past is behind us; the future is unknown. Between the two, on the thinnest slice of time imaginable, is the present.

The experience of living in the "now" is as simple or as complex as our inner lives allow. Few of us see each fleeting moment clearly or freely; its real nature is obscured by other concerns. The past, encompassing not only our history but also all of our past habits, lumbers along with us into the present. When we act, we are not sure if we are responding to the immediate demands of the situation or simply repeating a habit pattern independent of the uniqueness of the current moment. Anticipations press against the present and may further distort our view. We expect a certain kind of future and do what we can to ensure or modify it.

What if we were to view the past as our personal treasure trove of prior solutions—a record of events, ideas, speculations, mistakes and successes? We might then draw on that record to help us avoid new mistakes. To do again what has failed before is one definition of neurosis; it connotes not only an inability to use the past as a teacher, but the compulsion to recreate past problems and to live past failures. Neurosis is the part of us that hits our thumb, a second, a third, and even a fourth time when we aim for a nail.

A friend of mine was married, then divorced. He began to date, and finally started seeing a woman seriously. At that point he called to ask if I could recommend a therapist. I was surprised; this had been a man almost totally uninterested in his own mind. He had always said, "Life itself is psychology enough."

But now he told me, he was having the same problems with his new girlfriend that he had had with his wife. "They are totally different kinds of people," he said, "so it must be me. I want to stop the pattern before it ruins my relationship with someone I love." He had finally come to see that his past was devouring his present. Counseling with a psychotherapist soon made him more aware of his self-defeating habits, and suggested methods for overcoming them. He is now remarried quite happily.

The wonderful realization, the freeing revelation, is that the past is *over*—gone, finished, done with, completed, terminated—IF YOU WISH! You may, however, select out and continue to use whatever past behaviors may have worked for you, leaving the rest behind. New events should evoke new responses. Right now I'm writing this book on a word processor. I utilize most, but not all, of my typing habits; some are not useful on this machine. I have also developed new skills to utilize the special capacities of the computer. A friend has offered me a upgraded version of my computer. If I accept, I will once again keep some habits and modify or eliminate others. I will also have to learn some new ones.

The fact is that many experiences in our past are no longer useful. The secret is to separate the valuables from the trash, and constantly remind ourselves to use those valuables correctly. The future is unknown, but the way we establish our present has a profound influence on what it could be. The future is shaped by what happens in the present. The control of that shaping process calls for freedom from our past, as we choose. The future is too valuable to be allowed to come upon us by default, and too personal to let others establish for you.

THE POWER AND VALUE
OF SUGGESTION

The word "suggestion" comes from a root meaning "to carry," or "to bring to." Suggestion is the act and the art of bringing something to mind. Accepting a suggestion is to allow another to partly determine our view of the world. We may imagine ourselves to be self-determined; yet often we are simply failing to perceive the impact of external suggestions.

Suggestion plays a role in healing, which is a complex interplay between the body and the mind. The same forces that are trivialized to sell a product or a politician can be harnessed to benefit ourselves or others.

An example comes from Carl Simonton, M.D., who started working with the powers of the mind to supplement the medical treatments he was offering. While this idea had been given lip service in his own medical specialty (the treatment of cancer), it was not, then, part of the normal treatment procedures. His first experience working along these lines was with an older man with a throat tumor so large that the patient could barely swallow. Neither surgery nor radiation offered much hope. Simonton taught the patient to imagine his healing processes working successfully against the cancer. Fully trusting his young physician, the patient did as he was told. Within weeks, the tumor had begun to shrink, and continued to do so until it posed no further threat to his health. Awed by this result, Simonton applied this work to other cancer patients. If a patient was willing to do the mental work, the techniques he taught accelerated the healing.

Six months later, Simonton's first patient came in complaining about arthritis in his wrists, so painful and stiffened that he no longer enjoy fly-fishing. He asked Simonton if he should try the same methods, which had been given him for his cancer, to reduce calcium deposits and ease his pain. More out of hope than knowledge, Simonton encouraged him. Several months later, the grateful patient called in to report his great pleasure in being pain-free, and that he once again was enjoying fly-fishing.

Months passed, and he called again. He was sorry to bother the doctor, but couldn't help wondering. He'd been impotent for a number of years; perhaps there was a way to use what he had learned to overcome this problem as well? In his firmest medical voice, Simonton suggested a way to focus on the problem and was rewarded, months later, with a letter from a very pleased patient and his surprised and delighted spouse. Simonton has continued to extend and develop his work until it is now recognized and used by many medical groups as an adjunct to many conventional treatments when the situation and the patient's willingness lend themselves to it.

Another well documented case also concerns a man with terminal cancer and a different physician. A new chemical for his cancer was available, but only in experimental doses. The patient heard about it and begged his doctor to try it. The early results were remarkable. With each injection the cancer was reduced. The patient's overall vitality improved, and his spirits soared. Then a national magazine published a story calling the new chemical worthless—even a fraud. Within days of reading this, the patient had begun to regress; the tumor enlarged, and other vital signs declined. His physician thought long and hard. He finally advised the patient that he had personally talked with the investigator. The problem with the chemical had been overcome, and a new "super" version was being air-freighted to the hospital, The "new" chemical was duly injected, and almost instantly the patient resumed his rapid and dramatic recovery. What was the role of suggestion in this case? The second chemical was pure saline solution, nothing more, and the remission was due to the patient's developed capacity in using self-suggestion effectively in his healing.

Suggestion, in its most useful form, is the ability to put ideas into one's own mind to support health, work, and relationships. Self-suggestion, correctly used, is the basic tool to reinforce intentions and turn them into actuality.

For the mind not only observes, it also *creates* the world in which we live. By perceiving our desires and our beliefs more clearly, we open ourselves to remold parts of ourselves which help create the future we desire. The limits to this power are uncharted, but we do know that overcoming past barriers is as normal and as natural for human beings as it is for a tree to grow higher with each new spring. There is clearly more to the mind than any of us knows.

VI

THE HIGHER MIND

Mind engenders truth upon reality. . . .
In point of fact, the use of most of our thinking
is to help us change the world.
—WILLIAM JAMES

The alert *conscious* mind continually interacts with the external world. Through it runs a constant flow of sensations, images, thoughts, feelings, desires, and impulses—an unending series of observations and analyses of the world around us. The *subconscious* mind is a storehouse of memories, as well as the repository of our fundamental drives. It is here that minute to minute experiences are sorted and edited before they are either stored or brought into conscious awareness. The subconscious codifies the vast bulk of information acquired throughout our lives, which includes, as we have said, the repressed childhood memories that are often the genesis of restrictive habits—potential phobias, obsessions, and compulsions.

This now generally accepted model of conscious/subconscious was Freud's brilliant contribution to the better understanding of mental illness. The analysis of subconscious links between apparently unrelated conscious thoughts led to theories and therapies and endless elaborations of other mental structures. Freud's conclusions have been so incorporated into our thinking that most of us have no trouble with the concept of a personal subconscious.

As a practicing physician Freud was most interested in alleviating mental illness; his theories do not encompass the dynamics of the healthy, creative mind. Freud believed that physical and psychological disturbances were linked to impulses, drives, and fantasies originating in the subconscious. He concluded that mental activities such as dreams, fantasies, forgetfulness, and mistakes were ordinary forms of the same mechanisms that produced mental illness. While his theories helped unravel the tangles of the disturbed, disordered mind, neither he nor those who followed him did much to investigate the links between intuition, illumination, and creativity in normal consciousness.

Until recently, psychologists, preoccupied with pathology, almost completely neglected the entire area of the healthy mind. And so understanding the mental processes of gifted, talented, creative, or spiritually developed individuals has been slow in coming.

Freud's early model of the mind was only a beginning. While understanding the dynamics of the subconscious has improved our knowledge of pathology, and understanding the conscious has improved our knowledge of day-to-day thought processes, we still need to examine a higher aspect of consciousness—creative awareness—that uses both conscious and subconscious processes. It is often referred to as the Higher Self, or the Transpersonal—over and above normal consciousness, over and above the constraints of the conscious personality. A description of some of its functions will clarify certain aspects of the success process.

PSYCHOSYNTHESIS
AND THE WILL

Like many others, the Italian psychiatrist Roberto Assagioli, in the early years of this century, saw in Freud's work a gateway to better understand mental illness. Praising psychoanalysis for its successes, he nevertheless observed that it offered almost no explanation of the high levels of mental integration present in gifted individuals. Assagioli decided that there must be some *additional* aspect of mind beyond the conscious and the subconscious and that full psychological synthesis integrated the spiritual aspirations as well as biological and social needs. Healthy individuals were in constant development—growing, and actualizing many latent potentialities. Assagioli proposed that the *will* was "an essential function of the self and the necessary source or origin of all choices, decisions, and engagements." His work, called *psychosynthesis*, includes a careful analysis of the various functions of the healthy will which include deliberation, motivation, decision, affirmation, persistence, and execution. His therapeutic work involved various techniques for arousing, developing, strengthening, and "rightly directing" the will. He believed that a healthy and developed will was the key to increased personal freedom. To achieve this, he advocated active conscious participation, moving strongly away from the more passive psychoanalytic approach. His overall goal was to assist in "the conscious and *planned* reconstruction or re-creation of the personality." One should not, he felt, be content merely to eliminate neurotic patterns, one should also encourage aesthetic, ethical, religious, intuitional, and mystical states of consciousness. These, he said, "are real in the practical sense . . . because they are *effective* in producing changes both in the inner and outer worlds." He observed that to change our inner being beneficially, we must *plan* the changes we desire, *actively participate* in creating those changes, and *develop and utilize* not only our conscious and subconscious, but also our higher mental powers.

It is from the "higher self"—a higher aspect of the mind—Assagioli observed, that "we receive our higher intuition and inspirations—our artistic, philosophic, scientific, and ethical 'imperatives,' our urges to humanitarian and heroic action. It is the source of higher feelings, such as altruistic love, genius, and the states of contemplation, illumination, and ecstasy."

Carl Rogers, a well-known American psychologist, reinforced Assagioli's views in his descriptions of the attributes of the "fully functioning person," One role of the therapist, in Rogers' thinking, is to support the higher self in exerting its influence. "This newer approach relies more heavily on the individual drive towards growth, health and adjustment. [Therapy] is a matter of freeing [the client] for normal growth and development."

SELF-ACTUALIZATION

Abraham Maslow, the founder of humanistic psychology, amplified Rogers' therapeutic observations with his research findings which led him to propose a "new conception of human sickness and health" sharply contrasted to the more limited and pessimistic Freudian view. Maslow concluded that:

1. We have, each of us, an essential inner nature, which is to some degree natural, intrinsic, given, and in a certain sense, unchangeable or, at least, unchanging.

2. Our inner nature is in part unique and in part species-wide or universal.

3. It is possible to study this inner nature scientifically and to *discover*, not invent, what it is like.

4. This inner nature, as we know it, does not seem intrinsically evil, but rather neutral, or positively "good." What we call "evil" appears most often to be a reaction to frustration of this intrinsic nature.

5. This inner nature is not strong or overpowering. It is delicate and subtle, and easily overcome by *habit, cultural pressure, or hostile attitudes toward it.*

6. If this central core is denied or suppressed, we get sick—in ways that may not be obvious or immediate.

7. Even though delicate, this inner nature never disappears in the normal person—perhaps not even in the sick person. Though denied, it persists underground, forever pressing for actualization.

8. Since this inner nature is good rather than bad, it is better to bring it out and encourage it than to suppress it. If it guides our lives, we become healthy, fruitful, and happy.

THE GOOD LIFE

Our inner nature can be stifled, but not destroyed. Not only does it remain, but whenever we open ourselves up to it, it unfolds and becomes stronger. As we get in touch with this higher or transpersonal self, we enter a larger and more beautiful world, moving toward what Carl Rogers calls "the good life." The good life, says Rogers, "is the process of movement in a direction which the human organism selects when it is *inwardly free* to move in any direction." Rogers' observations of clients in therapy who regain substantial contact with their higher self is in accord with studies of healthy successful people. Rogers described what this contact seems to produce. It includes "*An increasing openness* away from the pole of defensiveness toward the pole of openness to experience." The individual is better able to listen to and experience what is going on inside and more free to be aware of feelings, subjectively, as they exist.

"*An increasing tendency to live fully in each moment*—an absence of rigidity, of tight organization, of the imposition of structure on experience. Instead, there is a maximum of adaptability."

An increasing trust in one's whole self. Individuals "discover to an ever-increasing degree that if they are open to their experience, doing what 'feels right' proves to be a competent and trustworthy guide to behavior which is truly satisfactory." No longer caught in past perceptions, they no longer rely on memories and previous experiences which confuse and cloud the present moment. They do not become infallible, but they tend to "give the best possible answer for the available data." Any errors, says Rogers, any initial behavior which is not satisfying, is soon corrected.

A person living the good life is naturally creative, not necessarily "adjusted" to the culture and almost certainly not a conformist. "Such a person would, I believe, be recognized by a student of evolution as the type most likely to adapt and survive under changing environmental conditions."

"The basic nature of the human being, when flowing freely, is constructive and trustworthy . . . I have little sympathy with the rather prevalent concept that man is basically irrational, and that his impulses, if not controlled, will lead to destruction of others and self. Man's behavior is exquisitely rational, moving with subtle and ordered complexity toward the goals the organism is endeavoring to achieve."

Rogers concludes, for these people, *"Life is richer and more satisfying.* . . . I believe it will have become evident why, for me, adjectives such as happy, contented, blissful, enjoyable, do not seem quite appropriate to any general description of this process I have called the good life, even though the person in this process would experience each one of these feelings at appropriate times. What seems more fitting are adjectives such as enriching, exciting, rewarding, challenging, and meaningful. This process of the good life is not, I am convinced, a life for the faint-hearted. It involves stretching and growing, of becoming more and more aware of one's potentialities."

THE HIGHER SELF IN ACTION

Assagioli, Rogers, and Maslow are early voices among an ever-growing number of theorists and therapists who agree that we are more than the sum of conscious and unconscious processes. Each described how we might function if more attuned to these capacities. While their conclusions were abstract, there exist descriptions of people acting from their higher self.

Here is Mozart writing to a friend: "When I am, as it were, completely myself, entirely alone and of good cheer . . . it is on such occasions that my ideas flow best and most abundantly. Whence and how they come I know not . . . All this fires my soul and, provided I am not disturbed, my subject enlarges itself, becomes methodized and defined, on the whole, though it be long, it stands almost complete and finished in my mind, so I can survey it, like a fine picture or a beautiful statue, at a glance. Nor do I hear in my imagination, the parts successively, but I hear them all at once."

Richard Wagner saw the ideas for his music arriving "like a flash of light in the greatest clarity and definiteness, but not altogether in complete detail." The French composer Saint-Saens said it most simply when he suggested that in order to compose, one had only to listen to those internal voices which spoke. In Beethoven's words, "The new and the original is born without one's thinking of it." These composers understood and used that higher part of their own minds to improve their conscious endeavors.

Great writers offer parallel descriptions on allowing or encouraging higher awareness. Charles Dickens stated, "Some beneficient power showed it all to me." Thackeray commented, "I have been surprised at the observation made by some of my characters. It seems as if an occult power was moving my pen."

Oliver Wendell Holmes' best ideas emerged from what he called the "underground workshop of thought." The English philosopher Bertrand Russell approached his work as follows: "My own belief is that a conscious thought may be planted in the subconscious [higher self] if a sufficient amount of vigor and intensity is put into it . . . I have found, for example, that if I have to write upon some rather difficult topic, the best plan is to think about it with very great intensity—the greatest intensity of which I am capable—for a few hours or days, and at the end of that time give orders, so to speak, that the work is to proceed underground. After some months I return consciously to the topic and find that the work has been done."

This aspect of the mind, which we are calling the higher self, touches some people through dreams. For several days, Louis Agassiz, a Harvard zoologist, had tried to classify an obscure fish fossil from the parts exposed in the stone slab in which it was embedded. Awakening one night from a dream of seeing the fish with its missing features restored, he went to his laboratory to see if his vision would help his work, but the fossil remained as obscure as ever. The next night he dreamed again of seeing the fish, but on awakening found that the images had left his mind. Hopeful, he put a pad and pencil beside his bed. His wife reported, "Toward morning the fish reappeared in his dream, with such distinctness that he no longer had any doubt as to zoological character. While still in perfect darkness, he traced these shapes onto a sheet of paper at his bedside.

"In the morning he was surprised to see, in his nocturnal sketch, features which he had thought it impossible for the fossil itself to reveal. He hastened to the Jardin des Plants and, with his drawing as a guide, carefully chiseled away the surface of the stone under which portions of the fish proved to be hidden. When wholly exposed, the fossil corresponded with his dream and his drawing, and he succeeded in classifying it with ease."

Other scientists have found answers to problems in dreams. James Watt finally solved the problem of how to cast lead shot after seeing tiny lead balls raining about him in a dream. Elias Howe could not determine how to position the needle in the first sewing machine, and took the solution from a dream. There are endless instances of solutions to long-standing problems appearing in dreams.

A different kind of dream solution suggests that the mind may have an even wider scope. After the death of the poet Dante, the manuscript containing the concluding verses of his *Paradiso* could not be found. After every plausible place had been searched, his sons decided to write lines to complete the poem. One son, Jacopo, then had a dream in which his father appeared and led him to a bedroom in another house. Touching a wall, he told his son, "What you have sought for so much is there." Accompanied by witnesses, Jacopo went to the house and to the room in question. In the wall, in a small niche hidden by a frame, were the lost final verses.

In hundreds of cases I've observed, properly attuned, people gain remarkable advantages using the *total mind* directly and with clear intent. Such examples are not rare, exotic events beyond the reach of most of us. Quite the opposite. Have you ever had a dream which foretold a future event? Over half the population of the United States report that they have. Have you ever thought about someone you had not seen in months or years, and that day answer a phone call and hear his or her voice? Perhaps you have thought of a distant friend only to have a letter arrive from them that day. It happens more often than we notice.

Even if you doubt the presence of these abilities in yourself, raise the question with a group of friends. I recall testing this idea at Stanford with first-year graduate students in psychology. A more hard-headed, rational, sensible, rigorous, and gifted group would be hard to find. After an initial wave of responses of "that's all nonsense, etc." I told a few personal stories. One after another, the students recalled similar events in their own lives or in the lives of their parents or grandparents. After the story-telling had gone around the room, I asked why they had all initially discredited it. Several students acknowledged that they trusted their own experiences, but had never felt free to share them with others because they were afraid of being ridiculed.

SELF-CONCEPT AND
THE HIGHER MIND

It is a well-kept secret that each of us has an active, functional higher mind. It is a delight to acknowledge this aspect of ourselves, and to learn how to use it more effectively. The higher mind has a vast capacity for solving problems, a capacity so well developed and so accurate that, when we finally perceive and appreciate it, we wonder why our lives have not been more fruitful till now. We need to understand why this flawless problem-solver of ours does not always make life as easy as it could.

What emerges is a strange but powerful truth. This accurate, inspired part of the mind is, despite its powers, without goals, without intention, and without any agenda of its own. It does not strive; it does not worry; it does not doubt; and it does not wish for nor regret the lack of any given success.

The level of success is limited and controlled by the level of conscious and unconscious self-concept. Even when people are highly motivated to resolve a problem, the effectiveness of their solution is *predetermined* by their opinion of their own abilities. Our level of achievement is a direct reflection of our attitudes about ourselves.

We do not get what we wish, but what we think we deserve. The mind is the bondservant of our self-concept. If your self-concept is low, opportunities for pleasure, success, and advancement will be deliberately overlooked. If you have a high self-concept, they will be noticed, grasped, and developed. This terribly significant and all too often overlooked linkage between two portions of the mind helps explain the life changes, career advancements, and "lucky breaks"—incidents that occur so often in the lives of successful people.

Lacking any agenda of its own, the powers of the higher conscious are still at the mercy of the limits of unconscious habit patterns. A man once told me that he knew his higher self was asleep on the job. "How do you know," I asked. "By the string of bad investments I've made over the years." He rolled off a list of investment disasters. No matter what he invested in, it would turn sour, and he lost money. His luck was so consistently poor, in fact, that it was remarkable. I asked him more about himself. He was a self-made man from an impoverished background and proud of his accomplishments. He spoke of his capacity to solve problems—how he had advanced himself through hard work and long hours. "But," he said, "I can never make a good investment—never!" I was startled by his tone—the same powerful, forceful, prideful tone in which he'd reported his accomplishments. His problem-solving capacity was anything but asleep; the problem his unconscious mind had assigned to his higher mind was *to find investments which would fail*. His self-concept required that he gain money only through deliberate, hands-on work. Investments seemed to him to be a way to gaining money *while avoiding work*. His long string of investments losses was, in fact, an inspired solution to the problem of maintaining his self-concept.

What are the critical factors? Achievements derived from contact with the higher mind begin with intention and proper orientation. A great deal of self-help and new age literature suggests that intention and orientation are enough. My own research leads me to insist that two other factors play a part. The first is obvious, although rarely mentioned, is that the bare necessities—the skills—must be available to the subconscious. People who cannot play a musical instrument do not become composers, no matter how pure their hearts or how strong their intentions. Second, this higher mind—the clear, bright, shining, creative, wise part of our selves—is a servant, not a master. It is employed by conscious awareness and serves us up to the highest level of self-concept that we maintain.

We can reach no higher than the goals we set and we will set goals no higher than we believe we deserve. In my high school geometry class, almost everyone cheated. The reasons were complex, but it was a full-participation, class-wide effort.

Our grades could have all been "A's" for we were not graded on a curve but on our test scores. But to my amazement, students who normally did A work in other classes ended up with an A in geometry as well; students who were B students handed in B work; and so on down to one individual, who, with the correct answers under his nose, almost failed the course. Each student did only the quality of work he or she expected to have done. Self-concept was a filter through which everyone's answers flowed and which remained as an internal governor modulating each person's level of success.

Our virtues coexist with our faults. How we can manage to act like a house divided, one part against another, may be understood by considering an idea of William James. In his book *The Varieties of Religious Experience*, he examined spiritual and religious phenomena, including what he described as the neurotic behaviors of saints. He observed that saintly individuals behaved badly at times—rudely, stupidly, selfishly, dishonestly. James searched for an explanation and concluded that *we have many selves*, many compartments of identity. Each compartment has a cluster of habits associated with it. He believed that if we do not pick one identify and hold fast to it, our behavior drifts from habit cluster to habit cluster, determined as much by outside forces as by our own will. It seemed to him that we should strengthen that single identity—consolidate it through conscious effort.

An appreciation of the scope and power of the higher self is an encouraging step toward the realization of our goals. The next few chapters offer a detailed look at problem-solving, sharing the wisdom and the ideas of gifted problem-solvers.

VII

PROBLEM-SOLVING

*To know
rather consists of opening out a way
whence the imprisoned splendor may escape
than in effecting entry for a light
supposed to be without.*
—ROBERT BROWNING

One can overcome almost any barrier, *provided one maintains the willingness to do so.* We are already superb problem-solvers. What *might* be lacking is experience, practice, or well-developed skills. Healthy children are natural problem-solvers; they seek out and revel in novel situations. Adults sometimes need help in reconnecting with their basic capacities—overcoming habits that block their original mental agility. *Essentially, we obstruct ourselves by believing that we are uncreative.* Only when this self-imposed limit is overcome can we start to develop new levels of skill.

First-class problem-solvers are well aware of the frustrating walls that so often spring up between them and potential solutions. As self-concept improves, however, one becomes more at ease with complex problems, can take on more creative projects, and investigate new avenues of self-expression. Each new arena, while it exposes new obstacles, presents new opportunities. Each of us needs to continually overcome inner habits which restrict the free flow of our creativity.

Even the most skilled and successful artists and inventors, the most proficient problem-solvers, need to address their inner barriers—be they emotional, cultural, environmental, intellectual, or perceptual. What follows are examples of each. As you read the descriptions, how many are immediately familiar—or can be found in your family or friends? *The first step on the road to change is recognition*—becoming more sensitive not only to the impediments within yourself, but in others as well.

EMOTIONAL BARRIERS

Emotional barriers are those feelings that interfere with your willingness or your ability to solve problems. They take many forms:

Lack of Challenge

Sometimes a problem seems too simple or obvious to hold your attention. It seems beneath your intelligence or the demands of your job; it's a task which should be delegated, put aside, let slide—something "anyone can do."

For example: my files for this book have grown unwieldy, and I need to restructure them. It is not a difficult task, but it is cumbersome and involves a series of small decisions, none of which interest me; more interesting problems are forever presenting themselves. The result is that the files are not put in order. Similarly I need a small brass fixture for a lamp which is broken. I know that I need to call around for the part, disassemble the lamp, check the new part to be sure that it fits and reassemble it. The time it will take to do the task, when I actually get around to it, will be under thirty minutes, including the calls and the drive to the store. The time it takes to overcome my lack of interest, however, will be (to date) almost three months. Meanwhile, the lamp stays broken.

We continually accumulate problems like these. The challenge is to learn why we are not more willing to solve them—why we procrastinate. Perhaps it is because there seems to be no learning involved, and thus no obvious challenge. It was said of Brother Lawrence, author of the medieval classic *The Practice of the Presence of God*, that although he never hurried and never worked quickly, he did twice as much work as any one else because *he always did exactly what needed to be done*. It is both a gift and a skill.

Need for Quick Answers

In a problem-solving group, you'll often find that certain members come up with solutions almost immediately. Once they find the key to a problem, they lock onto it and will not let go. Their need is to begin to implement a solution rather than continue to consider alternatives.

I used to admire them. Here were people who were already applying a solution before I could even decide if the solution they were going for was a good one. What I learned, however, was that the very speed of their achievement was a clue to a significant emotional barrier—fear. *The very existence of a problem disturbed them.* Such people are uncomfortable in a world with unsolved problems—a world of uncertainties. So they seek, therefore, not *the best* solution, but *any* solution that diminishes their anxiety. The need to flee from fear is, for them, the most pressing problem.

So what on the surface passes for quick-wittedness, or impatience, is often simply a lack of confidence. When you settle for patch jobs, quick fixes, or temporary solutions, you may be trying to avoid rather than trying to solve the problem.

Fear of Mistakes

One definition of life is that it is a process of making mistakes, learning, and making new mistakes. In problem-solving fear of making mistakes is a common stumbling block. It leads to doing nothing, waiting for someone else to take responsibility, allowing your ideas to be superseded—always reducing the possibility of a mistake, and thus reducing your fear. Unfortunately, this also lowers—to zero—your chances of finding a solution of which you can be proud. That being alive means you will make mistakes is not a cynical idea but a cheerful one; problem-solvers, inventors, creators, and artists make far more mistakes than the average person. They have to; they take far more risks. A willingness to take risks in one's work and in one's personal life is a recurring theme in the lives of creative people.

Here are rules of thumb for risk-takers:

1. If more than half of your ideas work the first time, your solutions are not very inventive. You are probably trying to avoid challenge.

2. If *everything* you do works, you are taking no risks at all.

3. If what you invent consistently fails, you are not learning from your mistakes.

A final examination I once gave took place on Lake Lagunita, on the Stanford campus. The task was to design, construct, and operate a vessel that would hold four students, cost no more than thirty dollars, and be able to go out to the middle of the lake on one surface and come back on a different face—safely. In addition to grades, there were two awards: one for the fastest vehicle to complete the course, the other for the most innovative. The final was well attended: five hundred spectators, including a local television news crew, girlfriends and boyfriends, rooting parties, bystanders, and the class itself. The exam, run as a race, was exciting and close. Any failure would be extremely visible.

The winning entry was a teardrop-shaped container built by a team with excellent mathematical skills as well as nautical experience. They left nothing to chance, testing their craft over and over in the week preceding the final. The most innovative craft was a true exercise in risk-taking, an open oval shaped like a ring with a twist in it. It was a Mobius strip, a mathematical construction which seems to have only one side. I had seen them made from a strip of paper as a curiosity; but had never seen one built to hold four excited and optimistic graduate students. They paddled out to the middle of the lake, turned it "inside out" and began to paddle back. Twenty yards from shore the frame broke and the whole contraption began to sink. Furious paddling almost made it to shore, but not quite. The design was brilliant, but it had not been welded properly; the stress of the race literally tore it apart. "How do you feel about your craft now?" I asked. It evolved that none of them had ever been sure that they make it even to the center of the lake.

It is to the bold that the rewards belong. No risks—no rewards. Real risk-taking assumes a self-concept which takes failures in stride and enjoys successes. Most inventions do not work the first or the tenth time; but to the inventor, each failure is merely a step on the way. Those who stop with an initial setback never taste the sweetness of eventual victory. A major American industrialist was asked how to be successful: his answer, "Increase your failure rate." It is a hard piece of advice to follow at first, but one which increases your chances for success.

The Desire for Order

A close cousin to the fear of risk-taking is a craving for order. Order is a sensible requirement in any large organization and in the lives of individuals; it becomes an obstacle when it interferes with creative responses. *Problems are exactly those issues that don't fit into any previous order.* People who thrive on order try to squash problems with rule books, manuals, and regulations; with tidy spaces, orderly files, and endless lists. Problems remain, but they go underground.

Have you ever been told that such and such "is not covered in the regulations." What you're being told is your problem asks for novel thinking—and you should therefore go away. Encountering this barrier, I've found that a direct appeal to the higher mind sometimes helps: "This is your special area; you understand it, and I don't. What would you do to solve this problem?" If they become reflective, you can relax—their problem-solving faculties are coming into play and they will search for a solution. If they reply with another version of "It's not in the regulations," ask for their supervisor, or anybody else, and try for the higher mind again.

At one point in college I saw that I would have great difficulty fulfilling a set of requirements before graduation. I went to the appropriate office and laid out the problem. The woman helping me studied it every which way. She agreed with me that there seemed to be no solution that would not cost me a lot of time and energy; but, she added, "That's just the way things are." In desperation I said, "Can you think of another way?" She shrugged and shook her head. Then, just for an instant, she asked herself for a solution. Her face suddenly cleared; she laughed and turned to me. "There is something you can do; take the classes you wish, then come back here six weeks before graduation. Someone will look over your transcript, see that it's too late to change anything, make an exception in your case, and O.K. you for graduation. Just one favor—when you come back, don't tell them where you got the idea." There are always solutions. They may not be comfortable or easy as that one was, but every problem has alternative paths.

Judgment

Often we prefer to judge ideas rather than develop them and make them work. This is a subtle barrier; in organizations it is often misperceived as a virtue. People who dominate by judging may be highly placed and highly paid, though seldom enjoyed or looked up to.

Can you recall being a member of a group struggling to solve a problem: anything from how to position a new product to where to hold a charity auction? As ideas emerged, one member of the group would continually shoot them down.

"We tried that three years ago; it cost us a bundle."

"You haven't taken into account the parking problems."

"We can't afford to create a new position."

"That vendor's no good; he's having delivery problems of his own."

There are also those who grudgingly acknowledge: "Yes, BUT . . . Yes, BUT . . ." These people, despite their wisdom and experience, are deadly "idea-snuffers." They are so determined and able to see defects that they rarely allow an idea to mature. If you observe them carefully, you'll realize that they're afraid— not only of making mistakes themselves, but of allowing others to make them. By focusing early, closely, and tightly on the defects in an idea, they prevent the initial proposal from evolving through a normal pattern of testing, modification, and improvement. Their premature criticism not only adds to the potential for failure, but reduces the capacity to create more satisfactory alternatives. It is easier to be a judge or a critic than an inventor, an innovative artist, a writer, or a flexible and creative manager. Almost every idea is born with rough edges, wrapped in false starts, and studded with mistaken assumptions. In its first stages, almost any idea can be belittled; but it can also almost always be improved.

What happens to a group if one member is an idea-snuffer? New thoughts flow at first, but their production gradually slows until it ceases entirely. The idea-snuffer bullies the part of us that is embarrassed when it makes mistakes. If every idea we come up with is held up and displayed as useless, we soon learn that it is less painful and less threatening to have no ideas than to present poorly received ones.

There is nothing wrong, of course, with critical judgment—if it can be modulated and not allowed to become destructive. It is said that a writer has two conflicting forces within him: a creator and a critic. If the creator is too strong, what is written is of poor quality; if the critic is too strong, nothing gets written at all. Successful writers achieve the right balance in widely varying ways. Anthony Trollope worked quickly, carefully, methodically, and rewrote very little. Leo Tolstoy rewrote each of his novels as many as seven times before letting it out of his hands. Even then, he edited his final proof sheets as heavily as he had revised the manuscripts. James Thurber's wife once looked at a story he was writing. "Thurber," she said, "this is high school stuff." "Wait till the sixth draft" was his reply.

Each of us knows the feeling of having an idea primed and ready to share when an inner voice says, "Wait. This idea will sound crazy. Reconsider." An inner battle begins. Sometimes the creator wins; but all too often the critic pushes the idea away and you say or do nothing.

Highly creative people burst with ideas. Often my engineering students worry about something they have invented as part of a class assignment. Will they lose the potential patent rights to the industrial sponsor or to the university? I ask them to evaluate their thinking process:

Is this going to be your last good idea?

If so, protect it by all means.

If not, enjoy the pleasure of creating.

Creative people are like fishermen; they all have stories of the big one that got away. The most creative are skilled fishermen; they catch a big one now and then. A friend of mine invented a product for a new company only to see the prototype fail at a crucial demonstration. The idea had been a good one; but the company never recovered. What did he do? He went literally next door to another small start-up company in the same building, created a new product for them, became their chief scientist, and helped them enter the marketplace with a product that was a stunning success. For him, a past setback was ancient history, just another learning experience he could use to improve his abilities for future projects.

For many of us, this is not the case. Failure frightens us so much that we hesitate to begin. *At the core of all emotional barriers lies fear.* Wrapped around that core are memories—some recalled, some repressed—of being judged and found lacking, as well as doubts about one's originality. When one is able to let go of past trauma through insight, self-examination, affirmations, or other techniques, these doubts lessen in intensity; the emotional barriers lift, more ideas become conscious, and creativity again flourishes.

CULTURAL BARRIERS

Too Intent on Preserving the Status Quo

One of the hallmarks of a successful culture is its striving for stability, predictability, and order. We need to belong and we find safety in a world that is regular, that runs this year the way it did last year. In a Peanuts cartoon, Linus weeps and wails about the disappearance of the snow. Lucy tells him it will come back next year. "You mean, winter comes back? I thought it was gone forever." We need a certain minimum amount of continuity.

But that need, carried too far, becomes a restriction. Consider these statements, heard in business meetings of some of my clients. Each one prevented a new idea, method, or approach from being tried:

"That's not for our department."

"We've always done it this way."

"I've like to have this reviewed by higher management."

"It's not in the budget."

"It's not in the budget" is one of the finest idea-killers available to unenlightened management. One test I use to determine the health of a company is to observe to what extent ideas not-in-the-budget are incorporated into on-going operations. By definition, new ideas *cannot* be in the budget. Tom Peters, in researching his book *In Search of Excellence*, found that innovative products tended to come from "the wrong people with the wrong backgrounds in the wrong department in the wrong division at the wrong time." In the most successful companies, this was true in almost every case.

"Don't be foolish," or "That's not logical."

These responses suggest that the idea has arisen in some-one's higher self. Ideas of real quality often seem illogical at their inception. They may at first seem like intruders—beggars at a formal dinner. Only after they are seated and allowed to speak are they found to be sound.

"That's not the way we do things here"—in this family, this department, this company.

An idea that reflects *the way things already are cannot be original.* By definition, new ways slash across accepted practices. A soft-ware company, for example, put out a product that allows one computer to send "mail" to another. The cost ? Ninety-nine cents. How could this be? For ninety-nine cents the buyer gets a disc of the program which allows fifteen letters to be sent. The program then stops itself and cannot be run again; if the user likes the service, the full package is available at full price. Histor-ically, that isn't the way things are done in the software industry which, while priding itself on innovation, nevertheless already has a culture replete with rules, methods, models, and normal ways of doing business. To creative people hearing "That's not the way we do it around here" is like waving a red cape at a bull. The challenge delights them; it's simply an opportunity—a new fence to go around, knock down, jump over, or design a gate for.

Cultural Restrictions

Cultures impose their own limits in the form of taboos. Every close-knit group has social rules: certain things are simply not done! In all human cultures there is a taboo against incest. There are taboos in many cultures against marrying one's second cousin, taboos in some social groups against swearing, taboos in some companies against wearing certain kinds of clothes. There are taboos about what can be said on radio, on television, in films, in books. Each set of cultural restrictions is well understood by the members of that group and completely unknown to newcomers. After the Vietnam war San Francisco became home to many Asian refugees, some of whom trapped the birds, squirrels, and other wild animals in the city's parks. They were amazed to learn that killing and eating these animals was not acceptable.

We all have inner taboos—barriers to areas in our awareness. We maintain these inner taboos to protect ourselves from the pain of difficult memories, shameful experiences, and facing our weaknesses. Such restrictions may indeed protect us from uncomfortable moments, but at a heavy price. Any area of the mind which we refuse to visit we are also refusing to use. *The more creative we allow ourselves to become, the more the mind serves us.*

I once gave a talk to a funeral society. It was a nonprofit group that helped people plan ahead to reduce unnecessary expenses and trauma for bereaved families. My higher self prompted me to make the talk a cheerful one, highlighting the incongruities in our culture about death and dying. It was well received by most of the group; but several people were offended. They said that it was wrong, wrong, wrong, to make light of anything linked to death. On the other hand, one woman taped the talk and later played it for her eighty-year-old mother. This led to their first real talk about aging and death: the mother was able to unburden herself about her own illness, and share her fears of dying. Understanding that going against a taboo can be dangerous does not put it off limits. It may be a storehouse of possible new ideas and the energy to activate them.

We all appreciate the benefit from living in a stable and predictable culture; but we should recognize that the limits which create that stability are arbitrary. At times, when the situation demands it, we need to be able to transcend those limits. "But that's impossible," says Alice to the Red Queen in *Alice Through the Looking Glass*. "My dear," the Queen responds, "I believe in at least six impossible things before breakfast." The Queen had her own way of staying flexible and open.

Take the case of the Wright brothers. They began their experiments at a time when both culture and conventional science insisted that powered flight was a violation of natural law. The United States Patent Office had actually turned down applications on the grounds that heavier-than-air flight was impossible. And so it was—until it was accomplished. Fortunately, one of the laws of nature appears to be that the higher mind does not assume, without verification, that anything is "impossible." A creative person tests out taboo areas, as a skater carefully tests the ice on a frozen lake.

ENVIRONMENTAL BARRIERS

Impediments to new ideas are not only internal. You are most free to be creative when you work in an atmosphere which supports freedom; creative potential can be impaired by a difficult or hostile environment. A number of external conditions have been shown to diminish or restrict creative output.

Job Insecurity

Dozens of real problems can make a job insecure—problems that have little or nothing to do with your own performance. A department, a company, a whole industry might be shaky. Business may be poor; new competition may be crowding your company's goods or services out of the market. There may be union troubles—industry-wide. Your supervisor may not want to promote you—or anyone else. You may be in an industry with high turnover. The net effect of insecurity is anxiety, regardless of who is responsible, and anxious employees are seldom creative. Our most basic needs include security and safety; stripped of them, we become cautious and defensive—far more liable to go by the book than to strive for improvements or innovations.

Closed-Minded Management

People in supervisory jobs often imagine that *they* are there to do the thinking, while those who report to them are there to carry out their commands. A marketer of technical products tells of a meeting called by his supervisor's boss to discuss what could be done to reverse a serious sales decline. "He told us he wanted the meeting 'to get our ideas and opinions.' But for over two hours, he talked almost nonstop. When anyone else tried to speak, he cut them off. He allowed no ideas other than his own, and it was his ideas that had gotten us into trouble." What were the results of the meeting? "I was angry and frustrated. I'm thinking of leaving." The man was talented, creative, with a zest for life. What he'd concluded was that his own creativity was unlikely to ever be considered. He enrolled in some classes, improved his skills, and soon went to work for another company.

Lack of Support for New Ideas

The authors of *In Search of Excellence* describe "product champions." These are individuals who envision a new idea, method, or product and fight for it. Many companies encourage this kind of crusading. Others shy away from letting people exceed their job responsibilities. While these companies may sporadically accept new ideas, they are less likely to keep really creative people.

Even in the most supportive company, a product champion needs high self-assurance to venture into the unknown. The corporate headquarters of a major insurance company hired a writer to update a series of manuals for their field offices. A new format had already been approved. The new writer found that the agreed-on format itself was outdated—far more so than the manuals he was supposed to be rewriting. He spoke with his supervisor, who told him that his job did not include revising the format. On his own he spent time roughing out a new format. He showed it to his supervisor and, with permission, to their mutual supervisor. Both liked it, and it was instituted. His job assignment was changed; so was his title, and, soon thereafter, his salary. If instead of pushing against the system, he'd accepted the initial defeat, what kind of satisfaction could he have derived from his subsequent work?

The larger and more formal an organizational structure, the more difficult it is for new ideas to find support. Many major corporations, aware of this, deliberately set up smaller internal entities to foster creativity. If you have a new idea, how is it first heard and evaluated? If the initial reaction is favorable, is there a way to move it further? If the initial reaction is unfavorable, is there another way to go? Finding ways to be sure that your ideas can flourish is necessary if the flow of those ideas is to be maintained.

Lack of Trust

We do our best when we have friends around us to cheer for us when we do well and to catch us should we falter. Ideas must be shared if they are to be put into practice. If you can't trust others, you will not share ideas, and if you don't share ideas, you will rarely generate them. How much you trust relates, of course, to how much you trust yourself, but is related as well to the level of trust around you. A supervisor who feels threatened may create an atmosphere of distrust where none has existed, thus destroying people's desire to help, support, and encourage one another.

Distractions

Not all environmental barriers have to do with other people. The physical environment is also important. Does it promote or preclude creativity? Industrial studies have found that when creative people are allowed to design their own work areas, they are concerned with the following, in order of importance:

privacy

extraneous noise

heat, cold, dust, etc.

access to equipment,

access to other people

The primary desire among creative people is to minimize interruptions, so they can do what they love best which is to work on problems—hard, and for long hours. They return to a problem again and again. To do this they need unbroken blocks of time so they can tease out aspects they missed on their first or second or tenth consideration. Some creative people prefer to work closely with others and thrive in groups. They form creative teams which have the same concerns as creative individuals. The group wants privacy, quiet, etc. Inside the team area, however, they usually prefer an open space where no one is more than a shout away.

Look at your own work environment. Is it designed to allow you to work creatively? If not, what changes might you make? Can you arrange to do some of your work where you have more privacy or more quiet? Can you arrange your hours to be more in tune with your own rhythms? If you are a manager, what can you do for those who work for you so that their work might be more creative as well? Can you establish priorities to keep the creative projects near the top? As you observe yourself and your own habits, see what is possible to ensure that your environment supports your own creative style.

INTELLECTUAL BARRIERS

Intellectual barriers limit information flow and lead to inadequate or inferior solutions. One obvious barrier is:

Incorrect or outdated information

Spotting incorrect or outdated information is extremely difficult once you are already deeply into the problem since, at some point, usually early on, one stops checking on basic assumptions. I once supervised some students who had been asked to design a new way to make changes on a computer screen using the keyboard. They began to work with great gusto, and soon came up with a fine idea which they reported to their sponsor. He sent them to a corporate researcher who told them that he had developed the same solution four years earlier. They returned to the problem, somewhat confused and a little discouraged, and came up with a second, hopefully novel solution. The sponsor referred them to another researcher who was filing a patent for an idea similar to theirs. Gloom precluded creative work for several weeks. I consoled, cajoled, and prodded; finally, they took the project on again. This time, however, they started by carefully reviewing the literature world-wide. Locating a promising area, their third idea proved totally original—a real breakthrough. It was immediately snapped up by the company for further development. Had they begun with the correct information, they might have made swifter progress and suffered fewer unnecessary defeats.

Limited Strategies

For motivated, creative people, the capacity to remain flexible and open to new approaches is a key concern. We all have our favorite ways of solving problems. We write them down; we sketch them; we tell others our ideas; we build models; we fantasize solutions; we make lists; and we dream. Our personal list of techniques is usually quite short. We never use all the available strategies any more than we play all available sports. Learning new strategies and new methods to solve problems can only benefit us.

Here is a way of extending your own list of ways of approaches that may work. Below you will find a list of some problem-solving strategies taken from the book *Tools for Change* published by Interaction Associates, a problem-solving consulting company. Consider a current problem in your life and decide which methods, (including those from this list) you would normally use to solve it. Then consider a few of the methods you would not usually use. Finally try to envision the difference in the variety and quality of your solutions.

Strategies

ADAPT	FORCE
ASSOCIATE	FOCUS
ASSUME	GENERALIZE
BUILD UP	INCUBATE
CHANGE	HYPOTHESIZE
CLARIFY	LIST
CLASSIFY	PLAN
COMBINE	RANDOMIZE
CYCLE	RECORD
DEFINE	SEARCH
DIAGRAM	TRANSFORM
DISPLAY	UNDERSTATE
DREAM	VERBALIZE
COMMIT	VISUALIZE
EXAGGERATE	WORK BACKWARD
EXPAND	

By becoming more aware of a wider range of strategies, you give yourself more freedom in solving problems as well as a greater understanding of the overall process of internal selection.

Using the Wrong Framework

Problems are often easier to grasp when words are replaced with drawings or mathematical formulas. Working with corporations, I illustrate this difference by producing a bag in which there is a block of wood cut in odd ways. One side is triangular; there is one square edge and each other surface has a chunk taken out of it. I ask the best communicator in the company—usually the president or the director of marketing to help me. He puts his hand inside the bag and tries to describe the shape that he is touching. I then ask the others to try to draw what is being described.

It is always a struggle for I am asking for a verbal description of a visual form. Most people don't describe shapes well; often the descriptions leave the group confused. I then allow questions; this usually makes the situation worse. Very creative executives, after false starts, have come up with ways to convey the information. After asking everyone to throw away their first tries, one asked listeners to think of the problem in geometric terms; he then began by describing each corner. Another successful presenter asked the group to imagine a huge cube of butter and then told his audience to slice bits of it away. Both of these approaches reframed the problem in a different language—one analytic, the other visual.

In discussing this exercise I ask people to consider what might happen when employees are expected to make changes in a part or a drawing, or a repair in the field, over the phone. At this point the group can see firsthand that using the improper frame for a problem is a risky business.

Consider a current business problem. Do you know whether to communicate or develop the problem through:

A written description?

A series of drawings?

A film or slide presentation?

Audio tapes?

Memos, models, or mock-ups?

Familiarity and skill with different languages expands the range of problems that you can enjoy and solve.

PERCEPTUAL BARRIERS

Perceptual barriers are psychological blinders that prevent the correct view of a problem at the outset. Because they render things invisible, they are among the most difficult barriers to be aware of in oneself. They include:

Seeing What You Expect

The loss of the ability to see freshly—to see with "beginners eyes"—occurs when we get too comfortable with one point of view, one set of beliefs, or one way of living our lives. A gentle word for this might be "preconceptions," a less gentle word is "prejudices." Notice if any of the following preconceptions sounds like you or anyone you know.

"Students are getting lazier every year."

"You can't trust lawyers."

"People can always be motivated by more money."

"It's useless to bring up such-and-such with him."

"She never listens."

"I don't have to taste it. I know it's yucky!"

We all have preconceptions—beliefs founded on inadequate knowledge, held even when reality contradicts them. We are familiar with racial prejudice and with stereotyping; it may also be apparent that restrictive habit patterns are personal preconceptions. "I can't . . ." prejudges our own capacity to handle a future event. It is a rigid mental structure that resists reality testing. You will not solve problems if you approach them "knowing" that you can't solve them.

"I haven't yet" is a more accurate description of the past than "I can't," and avoids perceptual blinding. If you must see only what you expect to see—a deep-seated human tendency— then at least consider what inventors and problem-solvers expect to see in a problem—namely, solutions or, at the least, the enjoyment of trying to solve them.

No one has ever said it better than Pogo: *"We have met the enemy and he is us."*

A Tendency to Limit the Problem

We all like to bring a problem down to size, but shrinking it sometimes prevents us from solving it at all. Our first impulse is to bring out our best tools and expertise to work toward a solution. And why not? Why not start with the skills and information we have and attack the problem directly?

There are, in fact, reasons for proceeding slowly at first, globally, even vaguely.

Consider this situation: a family is in conflict; each member is upset and angry with the others. How should one work toward understanding what is wrong? A physician might look for physical illnesses. A nutritionist might look for dietary imbalances. A psychologist might look for neurotic behavior. A social worker might focus on economic concerns. A relative might see patterns recalled from the previous generation. Each expert may offer to help. But there is a real risk that our "expert" eyes will *predetermine* what we see. Our own effectiveness may be impeded by our expertise—by the natural tendency to travel along familiar channels of thought and observation where we feel (and are) knowledgeable. "Expert" information often limits what can be seen. I have seen people work for years on a problem only to have it resolved in weeks when they turned for help to someone whose skills were more appropriate.

Most people know the story of the blind men who were led to an enclosure which held an elephant. None of them had ever encountered such a beast. Each approached it, touched it briefly, and came away.

"It is some kind of great stone pillar," said the first.

"Not at all," said the second. "It is a great sheet of leather."

"Absurd," said a third. "It is flexible thing with stiff broom straws on the end.

The fourth blind man laughed. "How foolish you all are. This thing was smooth, and cool, and hard as marble."

Had they been able to view the whole animal, they would have seen a leg, an ear, the tail, and a tusk. One cannot always perceive an elephant or anything else through the narrow slit of our experience, no matter how correctly we see through it.

As a general consultant, I am often asked to address a problem after a specialist has researched it, reported, and left. Rarely do I find the specialist other than knowledgeable; yet the problem remains. Specialists often are unable to step back from the problem since stepping back can be most uncomfortable, especially if you have to step outside your expertise.

Are we talking about you? Ask yourself: Is what I see the whole problem? Would someone else see it differently? If so, what might they see that I would overlook?

The simple act of restating a problem in a different way often casts light on initial blind spots as well as suggesting other solutions.

We all have barriers which obscure our view, past experiences which color our approach, environmental conditions which are less than optimal, and preconceptions which dull our clarity. People who are more successful than most have no less of these, but they are more aware of them, spend more energy in uncovering them, and have developed more strategies for circumventing them. Most important is that they believe in themselves and in the power of their minds to effectively pass through each barrier along their path.

VIII

OVERCOMING
BARRIERS

▲▲

There is nothing in the world
really beneficial
that does not lie
within the reach of an informed understanding
and a well directed pursuit.

—EDMUND BURKE

Fortunately, there are many ways to solve problems, and obviously, the more ways we know, the more versatile we become. Any problem-solving approach is a world in itself, so that this brief introduction is clearly just the tip of the iceberg—to encourage your continuing exploration. Let us first consider a theory about how we approach reality, and then attempt an overview of ways to approach individual problems.

WAYS OF THINKING

When we approach a problem, each of us favors one or more of the senses. Some of us use visual tools; our normal way of getting started is through graphic visual modes. When someone describes a problem, we respond by trying to *see* the problem clearly—to literally *look* at possible solutions.

Some of us are more auditory. We *listen* to problems, try to resonate with them, sound them out, and talk about them A third style is tactile, or physical. We try to *grasp* the essentials of a problem and wrestle with them until we force a solution. We build models, make projections, create alternatives. Problems are treated as if they were solid physical objects.

Our primary mode of problem-solving is always the best developed and most available for conscious use. Truly successful problem-solvers, however, are able to work in many modes; they more easily blend approaches, and are able to work with people whose dominant style differs from their own.

I am by habit a visualizer. I like to see things illustrated or written out. I take notes, make diagrams, create lists and envision answers. But over the years I have learned to work more with auditory and tactile approaches—to orally illustrate problems through story-telling and to use my hands as tools. I've become better able to repair things, and am in real contact with what's going on in my garden. I have been a member of teams operating machinery and have coached students in speaking skills, situations I would have avoided earlier. As a result, I am less afraid of problems which don't lend themselves to visual solutions.

When you work in a different mode, you are using "mind muscles" that aren't usually called into play. Having a choice of approach can make all the difference.

Sometimes the best approach is intellectual, abstract or analytical. Take this problem, as an example: if you take a sheet of paper and fold it over, the folded paper is twice the thickness of a single sheet. If you kept folding it over twenty-five times, how thick would the piece of paper be?

Method I. Approach the problem *tactilely*. Imagine yourself physically making fold after fold. How thick—in inches or in feet can you feel the paper getting?

Method II. Visualize the solution. *See* a huge sheet of paper being folded, getting thicker as it goes. How high can you see the folded sheet getting?

Method III. Analyze. Treat it as a mathematical problem. Let the thickness of paper = T. The first fold = 2 thicknesses or 2T. A second fold would be $2 \times 2T$, a third fold = $2 \times 2 \times 2 \times T$. Twenty-five folds would be 2 to the twenty-fifth power times T or 2×2 (the formula is H(height) = 2^nT)—an astonishingly large number. The folded paper is more than two miles high. Now revert for a moment back to the visual mode and you will see that visualizing those last few folds is extremely difficult.

With different strategies different solutions become plausible. Using a tactile strategy in this case obscured the problem; a visual approach was no better; a third way of considering the problem produced a solution.

Approaching a problem through multiple strategies until you find one lets you get hold of the entire elephant.

Can you identify your own favored strategies?

Can you find ways to extend your range?

ACTIVE PROBLEM-SOLVING

We tend to link the verb "solve" with the word "problem." But the verb, by itself, doesn't offer direction. Here is a rapid way to expand your flexibility. Let's take just one problem-solving strategy—"to clarify." By exploring some of the ways one can clarify, we can begin to see how far-reaching a change in strategies might become.

Ways to Clarify a Problem

By reflection

By illustration and definition

By amplifying inconsistencies

By comparing similarities

By questioning underlying assumptions

By locating points of difficulty

By questioning meanings of terms

By relating to feelings or behaviors

By summarizing a series of steps

By examining alternatives

By re-casting the problem in a different form

Each process can open another doorway. Should a solution elude you, step back a moment and choose another way to clarify this list. You will find this technique to be easy and astonishingly useful. Each new approach revitalizes your capacity. Best of all, practicing this kind of thinking can make you a faster and more creative problem-solver.

OPENNESS TO EXPERIENCE

Maslow studied individuals he called "self-actualizers"; the overall healthiest people he could find. He assumed they would be extremely creative. He also studied creative people, assuming that they would be mentally healthy. Neither proved to always be true.

He did find, of course, that healthy people are often creative and that creative people are often healthy; and what was common to both was an openness to experience. Moreover, both tended to see reality objectively rather than through the selective filters of prejudice, preconception, or restrictive habit patterns.

"Very frequently, it appeared that an essential aspect of self-actualizing creativeness was a special kind of perceptiveness exemplified by the child in the fable who saw that the emperor had no clothes on. These people can see the fresh, the raw, the concrete, the ideographic, as well as the generic, the abstract, the rubicized, the categorized and classified. Consequently they live more in the real world of nature than in the verbalized world of concepts, abstractions, expectations, beliefs and stereotypes that most people confuse with the real world . . . the creativeness was spontaneous, effortless, innocent, easy, a kind of freedom from stereotypes and cliches."

We can become more open to experience by lowering the barriers we erect to protect ourselves, and plunging more deeply into experience. I recall walking in San Francisco with the creator of *The Whole Earth Catalog*, Stewart Brand, who is also a gifted photographer. He kept exclaiming, "Look at that!" and pointing in a direction. I'd see just another city street, or a tangle of wires, or the edge of a building. But Stewart would be looking at the colorful couple sitting on the curb; a pattern of wires that evoked a musical staff with perched birds for notes; or the cornice of a building, its marble scrollwork turned rose colored by the afternoon sun. He showed me only what was already there; but he was teaching me to see more. Others can indeed help one see or hear or taste more vividly. Wine tasting with an expert; listening to music with a instrumentalist; going to a rodeo with a cowboy, or to a rock concert with a teenager—all of these enlarge one's world, and often enrich one's problem-solving capacity.

SOLUTIONS FROM ANYWHERE

Be open to unlikely possibilities. If you ask creative problem-solvers if they've had any surprises, you'll be assaulted with improbable story upon improbable story. A woman I know, just starting her own business, needed a certain kind of tape recorder. One day, in a pile of leaves near her home, she found a plastic bag holding just such a tape player plus a small calculator. She showed them to her accountant who said, "Wow, I've been looking for a calculator just like that!" Why is that a story about problem-solving, and not just about luck? Because there seems to be a large element of luck in the lives of creative people, and because this story is not untypical. Creative types seem to know how to manipulate the world so that more of the luck rolls into their pockets. Each may have their own approach; but they all maintain a high belief in their tendency to be lucky—a special optimism that is just another aspect of their overall high self-concept.

Here are two experiences which challenged me to re-examine where solutions come from and to expand my own realm of possibilities.

A woman I know wanted to visit Hong Kong. At a party she met an internationally respected photographer who had just been there. In their conversation she told him of her interest. He laughed, and asked if she could be ready to go the following day. She said, "Sure!" He then explained that he had, two days before, left a camera and several vital rolls of exposed films in a Hong Kong taxi. To complete the lucrative job he was on, he needed them within the week. They had been recovered but he couldn't have them mailed and risk delays in customs or damage to the camera and film. Twenty-four hours later, now the guest of the photographer's client, she landed in Hong Kong, a VIP to the airline and to the hotel featured in the upcoming photo-essay. She enjoyed the sights for five days and flew home to give her new friend his film, his camera, and her thanks.

The second story is about a woman who badly needed ten thousand dollars to restore her accounts after she'd incurred a once-in-a-lifetime expense which her income could not cover. As it happened, she was asked to consult on a book in a specialized area, for a rather modest fee. She did what was asked, sent off her findings and suggestions, and forgot about it. Two weeks later, in New York on business, she realized that she was not too far from the friend who had asked her to work on the book. She called his home, tracked him to his office, and finally reached him in the apartment of the publisher of the proposed book. As the three of them talked, she saw that she could have done a much better job had she known more about the project. She thought about offering to work with them that night; but she had no transportation; it was winter, and it was late. She asked where they were and found that it was nearby. Incredibly, it was the same building she was in and, on the same floor. It even opened into a back stairwell with the one she was in! A moment later, she crossed through her own kitchen, across the landing, and into the other kitchen. She suggested they review the structure of the proposed book and, by dawn, they had completely reworked it. On a hunch, she asked for a share of the royalties instead of a fee. The book sold over 150,000 copies; her share came to slightly over ten thousand dollars!

A DIRECT METHOD

Here is a simple yet effective procedure for solving problems. Each step may produce a solution. If it doesn't, proceed to the next.

1. Define the Problem—as Fully and Correctly as Possible.

A problem may resist solution because it is obscure, vague, or distorted. Writing it out may enable you to isolate the critical elements. The problem actually residing in the statement, "My daughter is getting so difficult and hard to live with," may become more accessible if you were to say, instead, "My daughter is staying out so late on weekends that she goes back to school worn out. Her work is slipping. When she stays up late trying to catch up, she gets sick." Defining the problem as clearly as possible, instead of allowing yourself to remain with generalizations, moves you that much closer to a solution or, at least, gives you an idea what direction to go.

2. Get Additional Information.

Some solutions await only a bit of new data, an additional resource, or a different expert. I tried for years to get one room in my house cooler in the summer until finally I asked someone in the construction business. He suggested a very simple way to vent my attic which hadn't occurred to me.

All new parents know the relief of learning that what they had considered a major problem (bed-wetting, nail-biting, sibling rivalry, etc.) is only a stage. Don't be unwilling to ask questions; the world is full of solutions.

3. Redefine the Problem to Yourself, Mentally.

With new information and another try at definition, many problems solve themselves. Understanding the problem more clearly sometimes let you see the obvious. A problem redefined often becomes a different problem—one more easily solved. But many remain even after one's best efforts. Restating a problem engages awareness and is a prelude for the next step.

4. Ask Yourself—Your Whole Self—to Consider the Problem and Conceive a Solution.

Doing this triggers the higher self and begins a process in which the higher self explores all available facets of the problem and then allows *your own inner voice, your own higher wisdom*, to speak to you. People who work this way get answers from dreams, sudden flashes of insight or occasionally in the form of an apparent voice, actually heard. This phenomenon is not uncommon with composers, writers, and inventors of which we've already spoken.

5. Turn Your Conscious Awareness to Other Activities.

The higher mind apparently refuses to function while the conscious mind is working on a problem. It is like a parent who resists helping while their child is struggling with a problem.

Only if the problem has clearly overwhelmed the child does such a parent step in.

Some people habitually "turn their problem over to a higher power." What actually happens is still a mystery. The ancient Greeks depicted the various creative arts as goddesses who, by looking with favor on certain individuals, enabled and empowered them to create works of great beauty. Christianity and the other world religions speak of the effective power of prayer. Contemporary psychology has its theories as well, which are not nearly as attractive as the poetic speculations of the early Greeks. There is clear evidence that some part of ourselves is there to help, if we truly want that help and have learned how to ask.

We have briefly examined a few ways to develop and enrich our own problem-solving capabilities. *We know that we can improve them—if we wish to improve* and we develop the necessary understanding. Problem-solvers are among the happiest people I know; they know that expanding one's skills is a joyful process. They delight in stretching their minds past prior limits; they delight in creating their own futures.

Having discussed ways in which the fully functioning mind might go about solving problems, let us turn to a more detailed examination of some of the basic goals we spoke of at the outset— health and relationships.

IX

HEALTH

The first wealth is health.
—RALPH WALDO EMERSON

Good health is a fundamental need. In childhood, most of us took good health for granted; times of ill-health always came as surprises. Slowly as we grow older and begin to have accidents, contract diseases, and encounter stress, we come to realize that health is largely an individual responsibility. Current research only underscores that we are the primary factor in improving or degrading our health.

In order to assert control over our health, we need to acknowledge the basic facts. Most of us allow too many pressures into our lives. We blindly accept the discomfort we feel, believing we have no alternative. It is true that we need to push our limits now and again to be fully human—to realize our potential. But while too little weakens us, too much can hurt us, and too often ruins us. Like athletes who alternate between hard and easy training, and sometimes rests, we need to be able to vary our own patterns, taking on more, and resting more fully, thus become healthier and recovering more swiftly from the inevitable stresses.

In your own life, can you identify situations where tensions accumulate? Is there any way you might begin to control these situations? Reducing tensions is a housekeeping job, like trimming ivy off the paths in a garden. The ivy, of course, continues to grow; new leaves soon crowd the path. Effective pruning—one key to good health—is an ongoing responsibility. Good health is a developed set of habits, not a series of events. While it may not always be easy, if you treat your body as a friend, and cater to its needs, it will usually reward you with a longer life. Treat it like a packhorse, overload it with the bulky gear of your career or your social life or your emotional problems, and it will eventually and inevitably collapse under you.

THE MIND-BODY CONNECTION

The mind's effects on the body are continual and complex. As you watch a horror film, you body reacts strongly as if under attack. Erotic images can cause a sexual response. Conversely, the body's impact on the mind is equally powerful. The most absorbing conversation will lose its luster when your head begins to throb or your stomach starts to ache. Should physical pain become a preoccupation, mental health also will suffer.

Each of us has, of course, a mental image of our physical body, and there are a host of interactions between the two. Usually the two overlap tightly; through training, however, you can learn separate the image from the physical at will, to your advantage.

Carl Simonton, in his initial work with cancer patients, mentioned earlier, found that when his patients *consciously created* an "image body" healthier than their physical body, their health improved. There is now plenty of evidence that if your image body is less healthy than your physical body, your health will decline. Compelling evidence of this from other cultures includes the phenomenon of "talking deaths." In these cases a powerful figure, usually a medicine man or shaman, publicly tells a person that he or she will become ill and die. The person soon begins to sicken, and within a short time the prediction becomes reality. When a Western physician looks up from your medical tests and charts and says that you will not get better, and have only so many months left to live, you may be putting yourself in the grip of a self-fulfilling prophecy that we now know has been scientifically verified. A strong enough belief in the doctor's wisdom affects the "will to live" both for recovery or for decline. In one study, a group of patients was told that the drug they were being given was a new and effective form of chemotherapy when the drug was, in fact, milk sugar. Forty percent of the group suffered the kind of hair loss associated with most forms of chemotherapy. The medicine man is a powerful authority figure whether he appears in a hospital or a tribal gathering and our capacity to implement suggestions is more powerful yet.

We can learn to correct incomplete or erroneous images of our inner workings and more easily maintain a high level of health. Teaching positive imaging to improve performance and health has been a rewarding part of my work since the early sixties. A few sports professionals demonstrated its worth in the seventies, and by the time of the Los Angeles Olympic Games in 1984, the idea had became widely accepted. A number of athletes recovering from operations or injuries which by conventional medical standards should have sidelined them completely won medals in those games.

Sports medicine and sports psychology are now studying not only the prevention of injuries and the elimination of pain, but also ways in which already healthy, aware, motivated individuals can continue to improve their physical condition. Learning imaging techniques to benefit long-term health is not limited to athletes or to athletic performance. From arthritis to diabetes, from cancer to the common cold, from walking to skydiving, from weight-lifting to fly-casting, imaging helps overcome limitations and increases vitality. In the references section a few suggestions are given on where to look for information and training.

STRESS AND CHANGE

To promote the intertwining of positive effort, increased leisure, improved health, and worldly success we need to understand the relationships between change, stress, and illness.

The research of Thomas Holmes has been invaluable in understanding the cumulative effects of stress. Holmes' initial observation was that the more changes there are in one's life, the greater the likelihood of serious physical illness. Holmes evaluated various life events, assigning to each a number of points reflecting its relative stress effect. The probability of serious illness increased as the total number of points increased. What is especially striking is that both negative and positive events added to total stress. For example, divorce is a high stress event (63 points on the Holmes scale), as is being fired from work (47 points). But marriage is also a stressful event (50 points), as is retirement (45 points).

From the body's point of view, it would seem that a change is a change is a change and that there is a limit to its capacity to adapt to new demands. A similar finding links major life events to weight gains. In people who tend to gain weight, during stressful periods weight goes up, and afterward, weight remains.

These findings caused me to take a closer look at the possible consequences of some work in which I was myself involved— work specifically designed to foster changes in people's lives. I conducted a research study on over seven thousand people who had taken a course I taught for Omega Seminars of Bellevue, Washington, and who were thus trained in the practice of the ideas discussed here. The research showed, as expected, that over half the participants had had major changes in their lives in the first few years following the course. The changes reported were predominately beneficial in nature: income went up (38 points on the Holmes scale), couples bought larger homes (20 points) with larger mortgages (31 points), more vacations (13 points), new jobs (36 points), more pregnancies (40 points), and achieved outstanding personal success (28 points). Desired changes to be sure, but such changes, as Holmes would score them, also added to overall stress. Might the work that I was doing, while it aided people in garnering successes, also set them up for major illnesses?

To my relief, one of the findings in my own study matched a later finding of Holmes. He observed that high correlations between stress and illness seemed to be true *only when people were unaware of the potential relationship between life changes and their health.* Understanding the links between change, stress, and illness and dealing with them consciously turned the correlations around. Holmes published a list of suggested preventive measures to counterbalance the negative impact of changes and for the "maintenance of your health and the prevention of illness." He suggested that people learn to perceive "change-events," understand their impact, and think of different ways to best adjust to the event. I concluded that one thing to encourage, as a way to improve overall health, is to balance each life change with appropriate physical improvements. Techniques for reducing stress, now widely available, lead to health enhancing habits as well as offering ways to reduce specific tensions. The combination of life-changes plus health changes adds up to a safe, happy, and long-lived future.

It's clear that much of early childhood is spent responding to the suggestions of parents, and that many of those suggestions, direct and indirect, have an impact on personality development. It has been demonstrated that adults can consciously reorient their systems, working directly with the words and images that have the most profound effects on children, so that even some long-term chronic disabilities begin to heal. For example, a Catholic nun had suffered for years from allergies and had to always carry a pouch of antihistamines, Kleenex, and nasal sprays. She learned a technique of working with the liberating phrases "I can" and "I don't have to" that brought her almost instant relief. She continued to refine that technique and, for the past fifteen years, has been symptom-free.

Although psychiatry and physical medicine are still separate specializations, one can no longer clearly define any illness

Holmes Stressful Events List

LIFE EVENT	POINTS
1. Death of spouse	100
2. Divorce	73
3. Marital separation	65
4. Detention in jail or other institution	63
5. Death of a close family member	63
6. Major personal injury or illness	53
7. Marriage	50
8. Being fired	47
9. Marital reconciliation	45
10. Retirement	45
11. Major change in the health or behavior of a family member	44
12. Pregnancy	40
13. Sexual difficulties	39
14. Gaining a new family member (through birth, adoption, relative moving in, etc.)	39
15. Major business readjustment (merger, reorganization, bankruptcy, etc.)	39
16. Major change in financial state (either positive or negative)	38
17. Death of a close friend	37
18. Changing to a different line of work	36
19. Major change in the number of arguments with spouse (either a lot more or less than usual regarding child-rearing, personal habits, etc.)	35
20. Taking on a mortgage greater than $10,000 (purchasing a home, business, etc.)	31
21. Foreclosure on a mortgage or loan	30
22. Major change in responsibilities at work (promotion, demotion, lateral transfer)	29
23. Son or daughter leaving home (marriage, attending-college, etc.)	29

24. In-law troubles   29

25. Outstanding personal achievement   28

26. Spouse beginning or ceasing work outside the home   26

27. Beginning or ceasing formal schooling   26

28. Major change in living conditions (building a new home, remodeling, deterioration of home or neighborhood)   25

29. Revision of personal habits (dress, manners, associations, etc.)   24

30. Troubles with work supervisor   23

31. Major change in working hours or conditions   20

32. Change in residence   20

33. Changing to a new school   20

34. Major change in type and/or amount of recreation   19

35. Major change in church activities (a lot more or less than usual)   19

36. Major change in social activities (clubs, dancing, movies, visiting, etc.)   18

37. Taking on a mortgage or loan less than $10,000 (purchasing a car, TV, freezer, etc.)   17

38. Major change in sleeping habits (a lot more or less sleep, or change in time of day when asleep)   16

39. Major change in number of family get-togethers   15

40. Major change in eating habits (a lot more or less food intake, or very different meal hours or surroundings)   15

41. Vacation   13

42. Christmas   12

43. Minor violations of the law (traffic tickets, jaywalking, disturbing the peace, etc.)   11

Source: Holmes, T.H., and Rahe, R.H. "The Social Readjustment Rating Scale." *Journal of Psychosomatic Research* 11 (1967): 213-218. (minor editing for clarity)

nor treat any illness as solely physical or only mental. Every illness is part of a larger syndrome which includes physical, social, environmental, psychological, and spiritual dimensions of the individual; therefore, reducing stress in any area will often improve overall health.

THE POWER OF WORDS

"In the beginning was the Word, and the Word was with God and the Word was God." What is it that gives words such power? Some Christian traditions relate that Jesus knew the "words of power" that could heal the sick and raise the dead. There are African tribes who believe that everything in this world has a living, active core—that people, animals, plants, thunderstorms, mountains, and rivers are alive. Words, too, are alive, being part of the cosmos; and, being alive, they are things of power.

In our culture, as well, we acknowledge the power of words. Some words are not to be spoken aloud within some groups; "Don't use that word!" is a common request. We protect ourselves after hearing or saying certain words: we cross ourselves, knock on wood, spit, or say a quick prayer—old forms that unconsciously acknowledge the dangerous power of certain words.

Some African societies see words as having the power to convert a spoken wish into a reality. Affirmations—positive present tense statements predicting a favorable future—are a version of this same idea, more familiar to us. Research shows that the power of words, while strongest in childhood, continues to affect us throughout our lives. Patients undergoing surgery under full anesthesia have demonstrated that they have not only heard what is being said, but have been impelled to react to it directly and physically after the operation. Research also confirms that patients told during surgery that they would recover easily without complications spent less time in intensive care after surgery and in the hospital overall than people who heard only music during a similar operation. We often see prophecies as curses or blessings evoking the power of words to affect personal health for better or worse. In some cultures, curses are used consciously and directly to harm others. We ourselves bless buildings, boats, meals, and one another. Even the words we speak to ourselves can affect our bodies; thus, it behooves us to be careful what we say about our health.

Should you tell yourself the following, what might be the anticipated effects on your health?

"As my Dad always said, 'When you turn forty, your belt needs to be bigger to hold your belly.' "

"You can never lose all the weight you've gained in pregnancy."

"I guess I'm getting too old to enjoy tennis anymore."

Now look at *these* sentences and their potential effects:

"As I understand myself better, it'll get easier and easier to control my weight."

"My eyesight seems to be improving when I do my vision exercises."

"People my age get extra pleasure out of being in shape."

"I don't eat desserts very often—don't feel the need."

There is no more powerful tool to help or harm ourselves, so readily available to each of us, as the words we speak.

THE PROBLEM OF PAIN

There are two general types of pain. *Instantaneous* pain is the body's early warning system designed to protect it from injury: touch your finger to a hot stove, and even before you consciously feel the heat, your hand jerks itself away. *Chronic* pain can result from injury or illness. When you sprain an ankle, it hurts instantly but then it continues to hurt to remind you to put less weight on it while it heals. Pain that persists beyond the time necessary for bruised or torn tissue to heal can become a condition in its own right and is a major medical concern.

Purely physical treatment methods such as drugs and surgery for chronic pain itself are often ineffective. The signals seem to shunt the gaps created through surgery and eventually override the dampening effects of pain-killers. The effectiveness of these methods may be temporary, even debilitating.

Pain clinics have been established to teach mental imaging, relaxation, and other alternative methods of pain control for non-specific pain and pain caused by a physical injury, operation, or illness. Patients are taught to expand their powers of self-control—observing themselves closely, learning how to control internal sensations and image their own bodies free of pain. Results can be striking. One clinic reported its results with patients who, before coming to the clinic, had had three or more operations for pain alone and were still incapacitated. After three weeks of intensive training, over 60% of these patients were able to resume full work, social, and family lives. The most successful patients had many of the same qualities we've seen in fine athletes, and in successful people in business or the arts—specifically, a high self-concept, a strong belief in their own capacities, and an eagerness, even a joy, when it came to learning.

It is your body's goal to stay well; you can do a great deal to help it. Good health is a state the body continuously and naturally attempts to maintain. By fueling work with coffee, staying up too late too often, reaching for relaxation through alcohol and drugs, one can exceed the body's capacity for recovery. By aligning the goals of your mind with those of your body, however, you can decrease tensions, minimize unnecessary pain, and alleviate long-standing health conditions. Before you explore solutions, you must come to believe that a health problem *can be solved*, partially at least, through your own efforts.

A middle-aged carpenter, a relative of mine, was injured in a car accident. He was told not to expect a full recovery. On his own, he began to explore body-work techniques, some of which were experimental, and as well as some simply not covered by his medical insurance. He found that he could indeed get help, but only by using his mind would his own healing be truly effective. Now, several years later, he has full use of all his limbs and "feels better than before the accident." Solutions to health problems use the same mental tools used to achieve other goals:

• Intention—planning to be in good health.

• Information—finding out how.

• Practice—doing it.

There is no one right way. The body is marvelously elastic and versatile; it can respond positively to rest, to effort, to passive or active work, to meditation or mental effort, to food or fasting. Find the ways you enjoy. Conventional medicine may often offer exactly what you need, and so may conventional nutrition; but there are also the diverse, wonderful worlds of sports medicine, holistic health, and health psychology. When you find the way that is right for you, you will know it—in your mind and in your body.

A Final Story

A college woman heard a talk I gave about overcoming limitations. She wrote me the following letter:

> I was really moved by your lecture . . . the analogy to running had personal meaning to me because I experienced success in running by shedding mental barriers. I'd never run more than three miles at a time; that seemed my limit. One day I entered a road race of four miles—primarily to get a free T-shirt. To my surprise, I came in second and so impressed a university cross-county coach that he offered to coach me through the sum-

mer. He encouraged me to run farther than I'd ever imagined possible. In the winter I began to train for a marathon with some other people on the track team . . . when I ran with them it was easy to say, "If they can do it, so can I." That spring I ran the twenty-six-mile race without stopping. My time was slow, but I was thrilled and ready to try another. (Marathons are great because they're not really races unless you're in the top ten. Everyone roots for everyone else and offers encouragement.) That summer I trained seriously for another marathon and got second place, demolishing my old time by a half hour. Elated by my marathon victory, I started cross-country again, knocked minutes off my five-thousand-meter time, and was one of the fifteen runners in the Western Athletic Conference to qualify for the nationals in Florida . . .

I don't think I possess any great physical talents; I just got caught up in a catalytic group of runners. We pushed away one anothers' mental barriers of distance and time—a kind of positive peer pressure. I think anyone can finish a marathon; it's just a matter of *convincing oneself* that five miles, ten miles, twenty miles are not impossible distances.

"No great physical talents." Perhaps that's so. What this young woman did have was motivation, acquired knowledge, daily practice, emotional support, and an evolving understanding of how to set goals. She trained her mind and body to work smoothly together to support her intentions, and was able to go for a series of ever higher goals. While her goals may be different from your own, she can serve as a reminder that if what you want is possible, and you know what you want, and are helped along the way, nothing should be able to stop you.

X

MARRIAGE

A good marriage is the highest art.
—OVID

Properly approached, there is no reason why marriages should not be superb. My files are filled with letters that include some variation of "Our marriage was O.K. before, but since we've been working on our goals and on ourselves, it's wonderful. "

Being a productive, creative, and successful individual is very fulfilling; yet for a partner in a marriage there are other goals equally or even more compelling. Economic ease, in any case, is not an end in itself; it is, at best, a foundation for a fuller life. Success that is limited to income, productivity, assets, and property is half-success. It doesn't necessarily includes the joys of good relationships with friends, parents, spouse, or children. Without caring relationships, material achievements lose much of their savor. There is no reason why our emotional partnerships should not be comforting and rewarding regardless of what else may be going on. And there is even less reason why such relationships should interfere with or restrict other successes.

Once, as a consultant to a company president, I laid out a proposal which allowed people a shorter work week. He looked at me and said, "I think you just want people to be happy; you don't give a damn about the bottom line." I replied, "If you don't think that happier, more comfortable people improve your bottom line, you don't know what helps make a better bottom line." Together we created a shorter work week—and ultimately a better bottom line.

In establishing new goals, it makes sense to review the state of our relationships. Whenever a family member improves his or her self-concept, the emotional fabric of the entire family undergoes a relaxation and an expansion. When we create change in our lives, the dynamics of our marriage change.

MARRIAGE IS YOUR RESPONSIBILITY

Marriage is our last, best chance to grow up.
—JOHN BARTH

After having spoken with hundreds of couples, I can safely say that most people think they know a number of ways in which their marriages might be improved. In most cases, however, each person can see *only how their spouse should change*, and how that would make things better for both of them.

There is usually real caring, clear perception, and genuine compassion in those realizations as far as they go.

"If she would only . . ."

"If he could, just once . . ."

Those sentences, completed in endless variations, are usually, true, absolutely valid, and stabbingly accurate. They usually have the right answers, but in the wrong direction. It is not, "What can he or she do to improve our marriage?" but "What can *I* do to improve our marriage?'' The answers to that question come more slowly and with hesitation—as if by speaking out they'd compromise themselves beyond redemption. For if one really knows and admits what one might do to make things better, the rational mind says, ''Well then, why aren't you doing it?'' It's a very difficult question!

The fact is that we all could be doing better if we had fewer restrictive habits and fears inhibiting our willingness and reducing our capacity for change. It is our lack of awareness of their present limits that makes us push our spouse to change. We don't see his or her hidden constrictions clearly nor our own. We wonder why he or she can't, or won't, do what we want; however, we know—even if we can't explain it—that whatever it is *we're* being asked to do is impossible. A quote from *A Course in Miracles* says it well: ''I am tempted to believe that I am upset because of *what other people do*, or because of circumstances and events which seem to be beyond my control. I may experience being upset as some form of anger, jealousy, resentment, depression. Actually all of these feelings represent some form of fear, and I have a choice . . .''

As self-concept strengthens, we are able to confront problems of our own, previously left unsolved. We develop new resources, strive for new goals. By correcting the imbalances within ourselves, and releasing our attachment to early limitations, our marriage can improve. Let's see how this can work.

TOWARD A BETTER MARRIAGE

> *A successful marriage is an edifice*
> *that must be rebuilt every day.*
> —ANDRE MAUROIS

In buying real estate, there are said to be only three important considerations: location, location, and location. In marriage, there are also three: communication, communication, and communication. Recent research, looking at thousands of marriages, suggests that a marriage is most likely to be seen as satisfying to both partners when communication is rated excellent; communication emerges as more important than financial, social, or even sexual compatibility. Marriage, (as perhaps all relationships) seems to follow some general rules as it moves from constriction toward more freedom. They includes the following:

Intention

Marriage is not a safe harbor, but an active voyage; intention keeps our hands on the wheel, so that as the winds change we correct and improve on how we treat each other. Maintaining a relationship is a continual, ongoing job of renewal. It is actually not so difficult: when we make improving a relationship a goal, *the intention itself* begins to energize the relationship. From that point on, there seems to be more energy available to uncover and solve the problems that emerge.

Believable Hope

Successful, thriving, vibrant marriages have much to teach us. Observe those couples whose marriages are as happy as you intend yours to be. Marriage is an art which can be studied, practiced, refined, and studied some more. Each stage of life brings its own mood to a marriage. Become aware of what makes a marriage wonderful in the first flush of love, when children arrive, during the middle years of career change, and in the later years, when the children have left, career slows, and as well in the final years when things are quieter. Each period demands new skills, and evokes new levels of understanding. Although marriage is not a subject one finds in any curriculum, it can still be learned.

Self-Concept

How much happiness do you deserve? The more you are willing to have, the more you are able to conceive of, the more you are likely to get. As in the other areas of our lives, we have a cluster of beliefs, many stockpiled since childhood, about relationships which deeply affect us. What are your own expectations of marriage? Do you envision it improving, staying the same, or declining as the years go on? Here, perhaps more than in any other part of our lives, we need to separate childhood observations and decisions from adult desires and goals. As self-concept matures, so will relationships.

Using What You Already Know

We already know many ways of improving marriage—or any relationship; the trick is to be able to *utilize* what one knows. If you feel blocked—unable to do what you know would help, why not ask yourself what else you need to learn. Your higher self is there, waiting for you to draw on it, and so are all the other tools, guides, and information you need. If you can learn to ask for support, guidance, and direction, they will be given to you. If you have not learned, that just means that you have one more goal to achieve. One way or another you can learn what you need to know.

Just as there are classes in child care for prospective parents, there are learnable skills which help marriages work. One of the wonderful things about marriage is that it offers ample opportunity to practice ways of relating—endless chances to overcome habits which limit loving and cherishing one another.

Carl Rogers, in a book exploring marriage, concludes that at the core of any long-term intimate relationship is an implied contract—a commitment to the idea that certain elements will be true as often as possible. Each element is part of an agreed-upon ideal for a continuing, beneficial, and meaningful relationship.

Rogers' pledge includes: [italics added]

Dedication of Commitment: "We each commit ourselves to *working together* on the changing process of our relationship, because that relationship is currently enriching our love and our life, and we wish it to grow."

Communication—the expression and acceptance of feelings: "I will *risk myself* by endeavoring to communicate any persistent feeling, positive or negative, to my partner—to the full depth that I understand it in myself—as a living part of me. Then I will risk further by trying to understand, with all the empathy I can bring to bear, his or her response, whether it is accusatory and critical or sharing or self-revealing."

Nonacceptance of roles: "We will live *by our own choices*, the deepest organismic sensings of which we are capable; we will not be shaped by the wishes, the rules, the roles which others are all too eager to thrust upon us."

Becoming a separate self: "I can be a real member of a partnership, because I am on the road to being a real person. And I am hopeful that I can encourage my partner to follow his or her own road to a unique personhood, which I would love to share."

Rogers' understanding, gained from a lifetime of counseling, is that marriage is a living, active, daily effort. It will work as well as we are willing to have it work. It flourishes best under the watchful care of two people who have learned that the pleasure of seeing your partner grow is equal to or greater than when you grow yourself. Like a team of matched horses, a good couple paces each other smoothly and easily. Sensitive to each other's needs, they enjoy moving ahead together.

XI

CHILDREN

*The more people have studied different
methods of bringing up children, the more they
have come to the conclusion that what good
mothers and fathers instinctively feel like doing
is usually best after all.*

—DR. BENJAMIN SPOCK

I n almost every home, parents do the best job they can. Every parent gives all the love, support, teaching, and encouragement that he or she has to give. Yet most parents, in spite of these best efforts, go through minor or major problem with their children.

Parents continually learn to *acknowledge*—and strive to transcend—their limitations. *A child cannot receive more of anything than parents have to give. Parents cannot give more love to their children than they can give to themselves.* Any limitations or restrictions which are the products of our own childhood, or any other source, are replayed in our parenting and may reemerge in our children. Similarly, any positive increase in our self-acceptance manifests itself in our children's behavior. Our children absorb our limits, confusions, and concerns as well as our intentions, capacities, and strengths.

Despite parents best intentions, children are often undernourished—not for food but for acceptance. Symptoms of "affection malnutrition" are not difficult to perceive, whether they arise from social or family difficulties, problems in school, or even ill health. But not all negative behaviors should be seen as a problem. Rebellion, at home or at school, against stupidity, cruelty, rigidity, or unkindness may reflect only sound judgment, self-reliance and a determination to make one's world a healthier one. It is when children rebel against useful rules, genuine affection, and helpful support that parents should rightfully be concerned and begin to take a close look at themselves as well as their children.

BASIC NEEDS

Aside from material security, children need:

love

attention

support

freedom

responsibility

Love

The need for love is paramount. Studies done during World War II found that some orphans, despite adequate food, shelter and care-taking, sickened, became stunted, suffered mental problems and died far more often than other similar orphans given the same material support but also given added affection from loving adults. That which we call love is an invisible, pervasive vitamin. Children thrive when given it and wither in its absence.

Recognizing love as fundamental is basic to understanding child rearing. Love is measured, not with a stopwatch or a soup spoon, but by the way a child feels. Children have an almost unlimited capacity to accept and absorb love.

Love, or the lack of it, is not necessarily reflected in either discipline or permissiveness. It is neither an act nor an activity. It is acceptance—absolute, without reservation, without demanding anything in return. As a recent mother said to me, "Some afternoons I get to love my baby daughter for hours at a time. She takes long naps so that nothing she does or I can do comes between me and loving her."

Attention

Attention is the second basic need of a developing child. Adults too require attention, but they are more able to seek it for themselves. Children need to know that they exist as people. What they say, think, or do is real to them and must receive some kind of recognition. "Children should be seen but not heard" is unhealthy advice. Children should be seen, heard, and attended to.

Giving a child attention does not mean saying or doing what the child wishes, and it does not necessarily involve playing, reading, or any other specific activity. It may be as simple as clearly noticing and reacting to what a child is thinking, saying or doing.

If you've ever watched a child trying to talk to a parent who's reading a newspaper, you've seen an example of a child asking for and failing to get attention. Contrast it with a child swinging high on a swing, joyfully shrieking, "Look-a-me, look-a-me," to a parent who follows every triumphant swoop or a child being comforted and holding a torn teddy bear or being held after being frightened by a loud noise. Attention assures your children that you are in contact with them, that you care, and that they matter and have a real place in the world.

We all prefer positive attention, but we can do well even when some of it is negative. Children that fail to get the attention they crave by being polite and well-behaved and doing well in school become rowdy and troublesome, perform poorly in class, or act out their frustrations at home. They need to be assured that they are cared about, even if it is only through being punished. What is often labeled "bad behavior" is often simply a plea for more attention and will vanish, not with punishment, but with more attention.

Support

The third need, parental support, is part love and part attention, yet it is not the same as either. One supports children by suggesting that it is safe for them to be in touch with their own special qualities—so they may experiment, stumble, and learn in their own way, without fearing the withdrawal of love or loss of attention. Families are most supportive and loving when they encourage children to explore the world as widely and deeply as possible, allowing as rich and complex a set of childhood experiences as safety and health allows.

Observe families whose children do remarkable and very mature things; in almost every case you will find parents who offer support in the form of time, energy, and if necessary, economic sacrifice. More often than not the activity is one that involves parents as well; the child is not only supported but guided. Families who play and practice music together produce a disproportionate number of professional musicians. Fine athletes are usually the children of athletic parents. Writers produce writers; chefs create chefs; doctors produce doctors; the parents of daredevils were often legends in their own time. Parents who give real support produce sons and daughters who take pleasure in achieving personal excellence. The quality of their eventual performance tends to reflect the high level of early support and encouragement.

Any developed skill boosts one's overall sense of competence, elevates self-image and encourages a willingness to take on new challenges. Researchers who've tracked gifted children over forty years have found that competence tended to breed competence. Children who performed well academically tended to be good athletes, related well socially, even had better musical skills—and maintained these advantages throughout their lives. The stereotype of the rigid engineer, the empty-headed beauty, the socially inept class "brain" is actually seldom found. The right kinds of encouragement can make children *generally* proficient; indeed much of the joy of parenting lies in watching and relishing the cumulative effects of parental support.

Freedom

Personal freedom, the fourth basic childhood need, is in many ways the most difficult to foster. Children are seldom truly free. They are not little angels come to earth; they are powerless small beings living in the shadow of large, powerful parents who control or influence almost every activity. From waking to eating to dressing to learning to sleeping, children have little personal freedom.

Parents usually walk a tightrope between using excessive control and allowing the right degree of freedom. We teach, make rules and demands, and reward specific behavior. At the same time we try to allow and permit children to make many of their own choices and decisions—to chart their own pathways. Ideally, we come to see that our goal is *not* to produce obedient, placid, well-mannered adults, but to develop independent, effective, powerful, individuals who are sensitive, sensible, and creative individuals.

I recall a time when my two daughters first visited my parents in Los Angeles on their own. They were young, and in our experience often unruly. After the trip my father spoke to me about their table manners. He was impressed at how polite and proper they had been at every meal. Surprised, I asked them how they had suddenly come to be such model children. They giggled and poked each other. "We made a game out of it," said the younger. "We knew it mattered to them," added the elder. They had the skills to be well-mannered when the situation called for it, and they were using the freedom they also knew to be theirs. Good behavior was not always their first choice—but when it suited the occasion, they would do it.

Having freedom is having the ability to choose, at any given moment, what is truly best to do; as well as having the capacity to do what you've chosen.

It is as important for children to feel that they have a wide range of choices as it is for them to behave "properly." My teenage daughter was standing in a subway train and felt a boy about her own age press against her. As she moved away she saw his hand was in her purse. She turned and punched him—hard, in the chest. The pickpocket whirled and fled. Her friends were bewildered; their usually well-mannered friend had turned and hit a stranger. My daughter's reaction was not exactly standard behavior, but it was right for the occasion. The sense of freedom we give our children helps develop the spontaneity and flexibility they need to respond fully to unforeseen difficulties, opportunities, and possibilities for pleasure.

Even well-meaning parents can cut subtle but deep inroads into a child's self-concept and thus into their sense of freedom. A woman in her early sixties worked with me to discover what lay behind her excessive fear of "falling down"—physically, mentally, or emotionally. All her adult life she had agonized over whether she was doing things properly or "falling down on the job." She had even avoided engaging in sports with her children, for fear she might fall. In the course of our work, she dredged up memories of learning to walk. She had been born prematurely, and her parents were always extremely careful with her. When she began to walk her mother was always there, laying down pillows beside her to cushion her falls. What she learned, along with walking, of course, was that "to fall" was very dangerous. The word and the idea eventually became generalized, until ultimately she came to be terrified at the prospect of any form of "falling"—falling behind in class, falling in play, falling from grace, falling in love. Once she became aware that her fears and habit patterns developed around them were the product of those early childhood experiences and from her parents' good intentions, she was able to free herself from those submerged fears that had troubled her all her life.

Another woman was working with me on a carpentry project. She found herself unable to nail a board into a corner; bending nail after nail. She started to weep with exasperation; then she became hysterical, and began to choke. I took her to a quiet spot and helped her follow her fear and choking into early memories. She recalled that her father usually became very upset when she cried: sometimes, when she could not stop, he would grab her throat to stifle her tears. She learned that crying led to being choked—to not being able to breathe. Therefore when she cried she became terrified. This early connection between tears and fear restricted her emotional life and affected her job, her marriage, and to some extent, her conduct with her own children.

George Bernard Shaw said that childhood is too precious to be wasted on the young; we might add that it may also be too dangerous for them to handle on their own. Childhood is a time of wonder, of love, of discovery; but it is also a time of doubts, fears and dangers. Children need protection—and they ask for it. They often need help in learning how to protect themselves.

Once I was up on a roof with a friend and his four-year-old son. One by one, we climbed down a ladder to the ground. The boy did it with great care and some help. His father looked at him proudly and said, "That was good. You're a big boy now." The child was clearly pleased with himself but he turned and looked up, way up, at the man towering over him. "No I'm not," he said, "I'm very little."

Children *are* little, and they get scared. Deep inside, they're not always sure there will be food, or shelter, or relief from things that hurt or frighten. Most of all, they're afraid, even without knowing it consciously, that their parents might not love them. Signs of childhood anxiety include nailbiting, thumb-sucking, holding on to a blanket, or a stuffed toy—normal responses to a world filled with unknowns. Before you consider persuading a child to give up a favorite but now tattered blanket, you should realize that it may be his or her very real comfort, an important defense against anxiety, just as a lucky piece or a religious medal may be an adult's way to feel secure and protected from the unknown. When children are relieved of childhood-generated fears, their anxieties diminish, and with them the need for additional security.

The best possible way to reduce the anxieties of a young child is to allow yourself to become a happier, freer, healthier person. You will be serving your child, first as a parent and second as a model. A mother, whom I worked with along these lines, was worried about her children who were becoming more and more jealous and argumentative. As she became less demanding and more consciously supportive of her children, the children almost immediately reflected her changes in their relationships with one another. One afternoon she overheard the youngest carefully explaining to the family dog why he shouldn't climb on the furniture, in the same tones she'd been teaching herself to use with her children.

I once asked a high-school girl why she was so intent on taking a seminar that I had geared primarily for parents and that her parents had recently attended. She replied, "Anything that can make Mom be a better mom is powerful stuff. I want it for myself."

Responsibility

The word means to have the ability, the capacity to respond. It is not a thing to be learned, like the multiplication tables, but a strength to be increased—beginning in childhood but extending throughout life. The greatest gift to give to children is to empower them through guidance, examples, and opportunities to master the skills that enable them to become responsible adults. From the toddler who says, "I'll do it myself," to the teenager setting his or her homework hours to the young adult decorating their first apartment after applying for and getting their first job, children want to be responsible. Every parent's goal should be to raise children who choose to be and are able to be responsible for their own actions.

Children are brought up in ways that reflect their parents expectations and are profoundly influenced, for better or worse, by the examples they see and hear at home. Thus, the first step in developing responsibility in children is to become a responsible adult, which includes both taking credit for your accomplishments and acknowledging your mistakes.

Over the years, parents who've improved their relationships with their kids have suggested specific ideas which helped their children and which, grateful for their help, I have passed on to others with considerable success.

Chores: It should be an axiom that everyone in the family helps. No one—neither parents nor children—should be seen as another's servant. Even younger children should have chores appropriate to their age and capacity. This helps turn the act of being helpful *into a habit*. A small child can empty a wastebasket, or bring in the paper, or help with some part of the kitchen work. For the very young ones doing real work is a source of great pride.

Be sure that each child understands his or her task. And be gentle; studies show that even adults rarely understand spoken directions the first time. Children learn easily when the teaching is done with clarity and love. Allow the repetition to form secure habits. Overly demanding parents can create anxiety and make the whole idea of learning something to be avoided.

Post a list of each person's chores, to make it clear that everyone has a job. For very young children, you can use drawings. Be sure to list or draw your own chores as well.

Parents agree that paying for chores is not a good practice. As one mother said, "*I'm* not paid for my chores, and neither are my kids. If something comes up that I would pay someone to do, I offer it first to my kids. That gives them the chance to accept it and earn the money—or turn it down."

Allowance: Children can be given an allowance as soon as they know enough not to trade their small dimes for large nickels. Having an allowance gives a child practice in using (and misusing) money and helps them to develop good habits—of saving, spending and planning ahead. An allowance should not be based on behavior, grades, or chores. It should be theirs.

As they grow older, the more of their own expenses they can anticipate and plan for, the more capable and careful children become about money. Ultimately an allowance should include their lunches, lessons, and bus fares, so they get used to paying their own bills.

When your children are teenagers, you can extend this principle to include clothes. If you can stand it—and parents find this a hard one—add what you would spend on clothes to their allowance. Let them understand that if they spend it on clothes that turn out to be mistakes, or they run out of money before their next allowance, that you will be sad and sorry for them—and that's all. If they are working, their money is their own, and their allowance should be considered as part of their total income. It is a delicate balance here, not to penalize an enterprising teenager by cutting back on their allowance because of their own wages.

Your hope, perverse at it may sound, is that your children will make some mistakes. It is so much better for a person to run out of money at age ten than to go bankrupt at age thirty.

My older daughter saved and saved from her small allowance to buy a skateboard. She shopped carefully and, after some months, acquired one. But, given the very rough and uneven nature of our streets, which have no sidewalks, it turned out to be almost worthless. She still remembers that mistake and, as an adult, is a careful buyer.

Two additional suggestions:

1. *Never give an advance.* This weakens everything else you are trying to do.

2. *Never pay for grades.* Reward a child with a treat, a dinner, a gift if you must; but treat school as a place where learning is the payoff. Good grades should come to be their own reward.

Rules and regulations. Kids want to know the rules—*your rules.* Hopefully they will be fair and impartial, and breaking them will lead to realistic, not excessive, punishment. Whether you are permissive or restrictive, your kids will play close to the edge of those rules, just as you did at their age.

Young children need firm guidelines. Rules for kids should be as reliable as gravity; otherwise, they will not learn to accurately anticipate the results of their actions.

Responsibility is developmental; it begins with learning to be responsible for one's own actions. In taking charge of your life, you learn not to blame others for what happens to you. A further stage occurs when you begin to be responsible to and for others. Children develop this sort of responsibility when they care for a pet, baby-sit, do some child care, or take care of some of the needs of an elderly relative.

The teen years are the time of discovering the dismaying complexity of being responsible to one's peers while not neglecting one's education or family obligations. Dating can teach what it means to be a real partner in a couple. Greater responsibilities emerge in adult life when people marry and become parents. Eventually, they find themselves parenting those who parented them—having to be aware of and responsive of the declining capacities of those who had once seemed invincible.

Being fully responsible means to have the clarity, the integrity, and the capacity to behave with care and compassion toward others while still keeping close touch with and honoring one's own continuing development.

SCHOOL

Other than parents, the most important influence in a child's life is school. From nursery school through graduate school, opportunities to develop or crush a child's potential abound. What can parents do to improve the school experience? The answer, from school teachers, administrators, and boards of education, is to actively and intelligently support your children, the teachers, and the school.

Support your child: *Visit your child's teachers.* Most teachers do the best job they can, but being a fine school teacher is not an easy job. Teachers are no different from the rest of us in that they respond best to attention and to appreciation. The more you acknowledge their efforts, the more they will support their students. You needn't always bring up problems or concerns or requests; it is enough to meet them and let them know you are a parent who cares. Let them know you will help them if you can.

I asked a junior-high-school teacher how he felt about parents who phoned or visited. His answer was sobering and instructive. "I teach almost two hundred children a day. The school's crowded, and we're understaffed. One year, just two sets of parents spoke to me about their children; I still remember those two kids."

It is puzzling that so few parents talk with the teachers directly. Your child may tell you that it is embarrassing—no one else's parents do it. That may be true, and it's all the more reason for you to reach out to your children's teachers to let them know you are actually interested in your children's development, as well as their grades.

Support the teacher: Just one teacher who understands the importance of improving self-concepts can leaven an entire school. In the course of a seminar I gave during her summer vacation, a nun who taught in a tough inner-city school learned how other teachers in other schools had successfully helped kids become more confident and have more self-respect. On her return, she was assigned a class of the most troubled and feared kids in the school. Quickly she found that almost every child carried a weapon. Four weeks later the last weapon had disappeared. By Christmas break she sent me a tape of the class performing an original song entitled, "I Like Myself." I have heard better voices, but no sweeter music. Another school teacher, now trained in self-concept work, asked for and was given the hard-core class—students too disruptive for most classes. After one year her class scored first in the school in their academic subjects.

Children whose self-concept is supported—by teachers and parents—*improve in school.* They direct their incredible store of energy toward substantial, life-affirming goals.

Support the school: It is possible to bring these principles into schools and school districts.

How good can a school be? At best, it can be like the elementary school near my home, where there are excellent relationships between teachers and students, and high academic test results without expensive supplemental programs. It can be a place where children get tearful before vacations, and cry at the end of the school year. "School makes me feel good all over. I don't want a vacation," sobbed one fifth grader. Graduates of this school regularly become leaders in the local high schools and do well in a wide range of colleges. Its faculty manifests a high regard for the integrity and individuality of each student, establishing a structured freedom that allows teachers to give each child love, attention, support, and endless opportunities for learning and growth. There are schools like this around the country, public and private—in the deep South and in Harlem, in the West and in New England. They differ in programs and outlooks; but each enjoys the strong emotional support of parents and the local community.

The lesson from these schools is that the children will learn if we do not stand in their way. They have an innate drive to master their world and come closer to succeeding in schools that respect this drive and allow it to flourish.

In Fairmont, Minnesota, the superintendent wanted to imbue the entire school system, city-wide, with these basic ideas. A day was decreed I LIKE MYSELF DAY, and set aside for in-service training. The children were excused; teachers of all levels and staffs convened at the high school for a day of workshops with the Catholic and the Lutheran schools joining in as well. Included too were the administrative, library, cafeteria, and custodial staffs. The intent was to develop a school system where everyone encouraged the development of every child.

The goals, as outlined in the superintendent's memo to faculty and staff, were as follows:

1. To help all staff members further identify with the idea of raising the self-concept of each individual student.

2. To ensure that the process of raising self-concept occurs within a framework of good discipline and mutual respect for one another.

3. To learn specific ways to raise one's self-concept and help those around us achieve the same goal.

The day did not revolutionize education in Fairmont; the system had been doing a good job. But some of the ideas included in this book were introduced and augmented the natural desire on everyone's part to help the children acquire a stronger sense of self that would serve them all their lives. The results:

less vandalism

higher scores on state examinations

fewer absences for both teachers and students

increased civic pride in the schools

A child's self-image is far more flexible than an adult's. It is easier to raise it; there are fewer years of restrictive habit patterns weighing it down. When teaching, I speak of "releasing a child's self-concept." Once parents and school allow the natural forces in their children free play, improvement in self-concept is swift and stable.

Just as they are easily made whole by words of encouragement and praise, children are easily wounded by verbal assaults. Untreated, these wounds lower self-concept in one area or another. If you ask your friends to talk about some of the skills they never developed—painting, music, dance, or writing—you will hear stories of a parent or teacher who had somehow communicated to them that their work was not any good. I cringe when I hear of teachers who have told small children that their pictures "don't look real," or "don't look like the one in the book." One result has been that some of these children stop drawing. Yet a stunted self-concept can be restored; creativity can be reignited.

One year, on the first day of class and without any warning, I asked my Stanford graduate engineering students to compose a twelve-line poem about love. From their initial reactions, you might have thought I had asked them to tear out their fingernails; no one in that class had written a poem since grade school. Their poems were subsequently reviewed by a popular and charismatic member of the English faculty who came to the class and read some of the best poems aloud, commenting on them and sharing her excitement. By the end of the semester, and without any further input, the students whose work had been singled out had continued to write poetry.

We are radiant beings! Look into any infant's eyes and you see pure potential. Even discouraged and thwarted, our children do not lose their capacities, nor do we. Full and natural growth can be re-established in families, in classrooms, in entire school systems. There is no age when we are too young or too old to reach for the stars.

XII

GO FOR IT—
NOW!

▲▲

No matter how qualified or deserving we are,
we will never reach a better life
until we can imagine it for ourselves
and allow ourselves to have it.
—RICHARD BACH

The following brief review is intended to create a bridge from the theory and ideas to an initial practical application. The most important test of this material must be— "Can it help me *now?*" The only way to get an answer is to test it in your own life.

We have:

- Considered and described the importance of goals—universal and personal.

- Described one way of looking at the mind—its forms, its structure.

- Identified a variety of limitations—inhibitions, compulsions, phobias, and mistaken beliefs.

- Offered what you need to achieve your goals effectively.

- Taken a tour of the "higher mind" to see how it can help your goals.

- Detailed barriers to achieving goals—emotional, cultural, environmental, intellectual, and perceptual.

- Presented ways successful creative people use to overcome their barriers.

- Looked, finally, at those parts of our lives which matter the most—health and relationships, especially marriage and children.

For each of us, *the time to get on with it is now.* This is the time to develop a series of goals which express your deeper needs. You—not the method—are the critical factor. If you reflect for a moment, you realize that you know enough about yourself, from your own past and from what you've read here, to go forward.

The following pages can enable you to clarify your own thoughts, and to make immediate progress toward your goals in each basic area.

I urge you to pick up a pencil and fill in the blanks or make a few notes as you read along. Anyone I worked with who actually took the time to think about and answer the questions below has had positive results.

As of this moment, you have a goal—and a chance to get it almost immediately.

Your goal right now is to decide—perhaps for the first time—what you want to become, and then to set goals that realistically conform to your innate, natural abilities and desires and thus—again, possibly for the first time—offer you another chance of achieving more lasting happiness. To decide which goals are right for you takes conscious effort and a new kind of thinking. In making the effort required to write goals and to describe the initial steps toward fulfillment, you put yourself into a new state of mind that will make what can start as a difficult job easier and easier.

If you do find it a struggle to write down your goals, you are simply experiencing a general truth: avoiding setting goals is, for many people, a recurrent habit which can be overcome with a small amount of conscious effort.

So let's start—first by asking some obvious and basic questions to focus in on a goal and then by following the answers to some natural conclusions and on to form an actual, immediate subgoal. In thinking about goals, freely include clearly short-term ones as well as those that may be life-long in their significance. Some will be easy to arrive at and to execute while some will seem unrealistic. Remember, "unrealistic" is only relative to where you start, not to where you can go.

BASIC GOALS

The Willingness to Be Happy

"I am my own best friend."

GOAL #1: How might I treat myself better?

_____

_____

_____

ORIENTATION: Are there any new skills or training I need for this?

_____

_____

_____

ORIENTATION: Which, if any, of my limits, or faults, or weakness am I willing to work on?

_____

_____

_____

What is one thing I might do *now* to make myself happier or more content?

_____

_____

_____

_____

One (small) thing I *will* do, as soon as I can, is:

_____

_____

_____

_____

IMPORTANT: Consider what you just did. *It was to open yourself up*—observe some of your limitations, acknowledge that you are willing to overcome them, and focus on areas where you *want* to make changes *right now*. Finally you agreed with yourself to *take action*—as soon as possible.

Work Effectiveness

"I enjoy working when I can perform at my own highest capacity."

ORIENTATION: What are some factors that lower my *productivity* or the *quality* of my work?

_____

_____

_____

_____

ORIENTATION: What are some factors that currently affect my morale at work? (positively and negatively)

_____

_____

_____

_____

GOAL #2: What is at least one thing I *could* do which would improve the overall value of my work?

_____

_____

_____

_____

One action I *will* take, as soon as possible, to improve my work is:

_____

_____

_____

Work Satisfaction

"I am proud of what I do, and I'm pleased that it is recognized by others."

ORIENTATION: Who knows what it is I really do?

1. _____

2. _____

3. _____

4. _____

ORIENTATION: How is my work currently evaluated?

_____

_____

_____

_____

What might be better ways or different ways to let me know what I'm doing well?

_____

_____

_____

_____

GOAL #3: What is one thing I might do to get more appreciation for the work I'm doing?

_____

_____

_____

One thing I *will* do to get more appreciation for myself is:

_____

_____

_____

IMPORTANT: I've never heard an employee—anywhere—say they were over-praised for their work. The above questions are to help you get more of what you need to do the work you enjoy well.

The Capacity to Love

"I am able, if I choose, to have good feelings about almost everyone."

ORIENTATION: My most important personal relationships are with:

_____

_____

_____

GOAL #4: What is one thing I *could* do to improve at least one of those relationships?

_____

_____

_____

The action I *will* take, as soon as possible is:

_____

_____

_____

IMPORTANT: This may be to do no more than send a card, make a phone call, or say a passing word or two. It is easy to underestimate how much even a small gesture can mean to someone else.

**Not all relationships are nourishing.
Sometimes we need to help ourselves end
relationships—to help everyone involved.**

Is there a relationship you'd rather be done with?

_____

Is there something you might do to make it end sooner or easier?

_____

_____

One step I'm *willing* to take as soon as possible is:

_____

_____

Good Health

**"I love my body, and I am aware of what I
need to do to stay healthy."**

ORIENTATION: What are your best health habits? What are you doing that improves your health?

_____

_____

ORIENTATION: What are you doing that is not good for your health?

_____

_____

_____

GOAL #5: What is one thing you *could* do to improve your health and extend your life?

_____

_____

_____

_____

One thing I *will* do, as soon as possible, to improve my health is:

_____

_____

_____

Inner Integrity

**"I have the freedom to decide my own actions;
I am responsible for my own life."**

ORIENTATION: Where in your daily life, at work or at home, do you feel restricted, constrained, hedged in, doing what others have laid out for you to do?

_____

_____

_____

ORIENTATION: Are you doing the kind of work you want to be doing? If not, what would you rather do?

_____

_____

GOAL #6: What is one thing you *might* do to gain more control over your inner or your outer life, to do more of what you want to do?

_____

_____

One action I *will* take, as soon as possible, to gain more control of my life is:

_____

_____

_____

If you know

where you want to go

and are determined to get there,

nothing

can prevent

you—

once you are

willing to start,

willing to continue,

and willing to deserve

the rewards.

AFTERWORD

Quality is never an accident;
it is always the result of intelligent effort.
—JOHN RUSKIN

A KEY TO UNDERSTANDING
AND USING SELF-
IMPROVEMENT SYSTEMS

O ver the past twenty years I have researched, partici-
pated in and conducted classes using and contrasting
dozens of self-help systems. Each year a new crop
of self-help books appears. Each book and each system has a
different emphasis, a different flavor. Some highlight material
success, some spiritual goals, many deal with relationships, and
a growing number focus on health.

More recently there has been a wave of audio tapes which
generally cover the same materials as the books and add exercises for relaxation, stress reduction, image formation, and specific
confrontation of problems including obesity, smoking, shyness
and insomnia.

And there are now video tapes available offering all of the above plus vivid visual sequences designed to improve skills—closing a sale, cooking a meal, sailing a boat or lowering your golf score.

There are three things which may help you decide which of these offerings or which parts of them might be helpful to you—the person you are—among them all.

1. Almost all the programs will work! If you read the books, or listen to the tapes, or play the videos—and follow the suggestions offered, you will probably be helped. You'll know within a few minutes if a program has something right for you. Trust your instincts! Those that are essentially inspirational may motivate—usually briefly, sometimes deeply; the more practical ones will give you a few new ways to work with yourself and with the world. As most of the presentations are variations around a common theme, most are sensible, tested at least by their creators, and have some track record before being published.

2. No program will work—unless *you* are willing to change. The purpose of this book is to help you set goals, be more comfortable with change, more aware of the obstacles within you which resist change, and better equipped to overcome them.

3. Almost all of the self-help literature, despite wide variations in approach, *describes the same processes.* A few include extra steps, a few leave out a step or two; but the bulk of the self-help material is based on the same progression to teach you to move or take you from one state of personal development to the next. Each step—*when fully experienced*—provides you the information, ideas, and practices which you need to go on.

What follows is a key to most self-help material currently available—from the deeply religious texts to the video tapes designed to improve bowling skills. It is a formal list: on one side there are the internal feelings that commonly accompany each step and across from it an abstract term—a different way of stating the same information. When I am trying to understand a new system or any form of helping, I sometimes use the statements and the objective terms as a template to lay over the system to see where it is strongest and what aspects it emphasizes.

From Wish to Fact:
Steps in Setting and Getting Goals[1]

THE INNER STATEMENTS	THE STEPS

Initial Desire

I want	INTENTION

Internal Reorganization

I am . . . I can . . . I do . . .	AFFIRMATIONS
I see myself doing	VISUALIZATION
It feels wonderful	EMOTIONALIZATION

Orientation

This is the right direction	EXTERNAL ORIENTATION
I understand	COMPREHENSION
• I observe	of the SITUATION
• Why not now and why not easily?	COMPREHENSION of the LIMITATIONS
I know what is real	External Limits
This is all I can do	Personal Limits

Initial Activity

I have started	ACTIVATION

---

[1]This sequence created with the help of Richard Moore

Knowing these steps can make it easier for you to use different methods and to appreciate the relationships between different systems of ideas.

This book has been one way of going through these steps.

This is the end of one cycle, and the beginning of the next. You have the knowledge; you know the steps, you have the tools. Will you make the commitment? Whenever you say; you're ready—that moment you start.

Go for it!

SELECTED
REFERENCES

†Adams, James. *Conceptual Blockbusting: A Guide to Better Ideas* (Second Edition). Norton, New York, 1980.

†Albrecht, Karl. *Brain Power: Learn to Improve Your Thinking Skills.* Prentice-Hall, New Jersey, 1980.

Assagioli, Roberto. *Psychosynthesis: A Manual of Principles and Techniques.* Penguin Books, New York, 1971.

Assagioli, Roberto. *The Act of Will.* Viking Press, New York, 1973.

A Course in Miracles. Foundation for Inner Peace, Tiburon, California, 1975.

Barth, John. *The Floating Opera.* Avon Books, New York, 1956.

Bandler, Richard and Grinder, John. *The Structure of Magic,* Volume 1. Science and Behavior, Palo Alto, California, 1976.

Brown, Molly Young. *The Unfolding Self.* Psychosynthesis Press, Los Angeles, 1983.

Cameron-Bandler, Leslie. *They Lived Happily Ever After.* Meta, Cupertino, California, 1978.

‡Davis, Ken and Taylor, Tom. *Kids and Cash: Solving a Parent's Dilemma.* Oak Tree, La Jolla, California, 1979.

†Book related to problem-solving.
*Book related to health.
‡Book related to children.

‡Dodson, Fitzhugh. *How to Parent.* New American Library, New York, 1971.

†Dychtwald, Ken. *Body-Mind.* Jove, New York, 1978.

Fadiman, James. "You and Your Attitudes" in *You Are Somebody Special.* Charlie Shedd (Ed.). McGraw-Hill, New York, 1982, pp. 37–59.

‡Felker, Donald. *Helping Children to Like Themselves.* Burgess, Minneapolis, Minnesota, 1979.

Ferrucci, Piero. *What We May Be.* Tarcher, Los Angeles, 1982.

Frager, Robert and Fadiman, James. *Personality and Personal Growth* (Second Edition). Harper & Row, New York, 1984.

Gawain, Shakti. *Creative Visualization.* Bantam Books, New York, 1982.

†Hanks, Kurt and Parry, Jay A. *Wake Up Your Creative Genius.* Kaufmann, Los Altos, California, 1983.

*Holmes, Thomas H. "Stress: The New Etiology" in *Health for the Whole Person.* Hastings, A, Fadiman, J. and Gordon, J. (Eds). Westview Press, Boulder, Colorado, 1980, pp. 345–362.

*Holmes, Thomas H. and Rahe, R.H. "The Social Readjustment Rating Scale." *Journal of Psychosomatic Research*, 1967, 11, pp. 213–218.

Horney, Karen. "Finding the Real Self." *American Journal of Psychoanalysis*, 1949, 9:3.

†Interaction Associates. *Tools for Change* (Second Edition). Interaction, San Francisco, 1970.

James, William. *The Principles of Psychology.* Holt, Rinehart & Winston, New York, 1890.

James, William, *Talks to Teachers.* Holt, Rinehart & Winston, New York, 1899.

James, William. *The Energies of Men.* Dodd, Mead, New York, 1926.

James, William. *Varieties of Religious Experience.* Mentor, New York, 1958.

Lowry, R. (Ed.). *Dominance, Self-esteem, Self-actualization: Germinal Papers of A.H. Maslow.* Brooks/Cole, Monterey, California, 1973.

†Maier, Norman. *Problem Solving and Creativity in Individuals and Groups.* Brooks/Cole, Monterey, California. 1970.

Maslow, A.H. *Toward a Psychology of Being.* Van Nostrand, New York, 1968.

Maslow, A.H. *Motivation and Personality* (Third Edition). Harper & Row, New York, 1987.

Orage, A.R. *Psychological Exercises and Essays.* Janus, London, 1965.

*Pelletier, Kenneth R. *Mind As Healer, Mind As Slayer: A Holistic Approach to Preventing Stress Disorders.* Delta, New York, 1977.

Peters, Thomas J. and Waterman, Robert H., Jr. *In Search of Excellence.* Warner Books, New York, 1984.

Ray, Sondra. *I Deserve Love.* Celestial Arts, Berkeley, California, 1976.

Rogers, Carl. *On Becoming a Person.* Houghton Mifflin, Boston, 1961.

Rogers, Carl. *Carl Rogers on Encounter Groups.* Harper & Row, New York, 1970.

Rogers, Carl. *Becoming Partners: Marriage and Its Alternatives.* Dell, New York, 1972.

Rosen, Sidney. *My Voice Will Go with You: The Teaching Tales of Milton Erikson.* Norton, New York, 1982.

Samuels, Mike and Samuels, Nancy. *Seeing with the Mind's Eye: The History, Technique and Uses of Visualization.* Random House-Bookworks, New York–Berkeley, 1975.

*Simonton, O. Carl, Simonton-Matthews, Stephanie and Creighton, James. *Getting Well Again.* Tarcher, Los Angeles, 1981.

†van Oech, Roger. *A Whack on the Side of the Head.* Creative Think, Menlo Park, California, 1982.

INDEX